1981

Merry

xxx
Janet, Gil
+
Erich

Railways at War

Railways at War

John Westwood

San Diego Howell-North Books California

First published in 1980 by
Osprey Publishing Limited.
12-14 Long Acre. London WC2EgLP
A Member Company of the
George Philip Group

First American Edition
Manufactured in the United States of America

For information write to:
Howell-North Books
P.O. Box 3051
La Jolla, California 92038

Library of Congress Cataloging in Publication Data

  Westwood, John, 1931-
    Railways at war.

    Includes index.
    1. Railroads — History—20th century. 2. World
politics—20th century.   I. Title.
HE1021.W47   1981   385'.09'04   80-25429
ISBN 0-8310-7138-9

1 2 3 4 5 6 7 8 9   84 83 82 81 80

Contents

Chapter I

Early Railways and the Military

'Well done steam! Smoke, thou art wonderful, and a reformer!' General Sir Charles Napier exulted in his diary of 1839. Summoned from his northern headquarters to discuss how to quell a threatened rebellion, he had presented himself to Lord John Russell in London within twenty-four hours of receiving the message, thanks to the newly opened Grand Junction and London & Birmingham railways. A few weeks later, as he brought in troops to suppress a rising feared in Manchester, he had further occasion to bless the railways, this time the Liverpool & Manchester line. The 10th Regiment of Foot, sent from Ireland, was in Manchester only a few hours after disembarking at Liverpool. Not only were the reinforcements fresh but the Railway had produced an unexpected bonus for the hard-pressed Sir Charles: 'One wing of the 10th came by morning train yesterday: the other by an evening train, which made everybody suppose two regiments had arrived.'

Soon after its opening in 1830, the Liverpool & Manchester Railway had been the first to carry troops on active service, when urgent reinforcements were sent to Ireland from Manchester; the rail journey to Liverpool was said to have saved two days' marching. This Railway was also the first to have an agreement with the government on special cheap fares for troops; in the early 1840s a new but similar agreement was made between the government and all other British railways, the fare being $2\frac{1}{8}$ pence per mile. Such fares were lower than standard rates and, moreover, the War Office saved the extra expense incurred by a soldier on the march, reckoned at about one shilling per day (most of which found its way into roadside inns).

Britain was thus a pioneer in the use of existing railways for troop movements and also, perhaps, for stores; the army established a large ordnance depot at Weedon in 1844 solely because that town was on the London & Birmingham Railway. Britain was also the first to build a railway for purely military reasons; the line supplying the expeditionary forces in Russia during the Crimean War was laid by British navvies in 1855. It was a primitive railway, running between the Allied encampments outside Sevastopol and the supply harbour of Balaclava. Six miles in length, the line was worked by steam locomotives at the harbour end and by horses elsewhere, except for a section where the tip-up wagons moved by gravity. By the end of the war this line, served by about a thousand British and Turkish workers, proved capable of carrying 700 tons of traffic daily, thereby saving about 4,000 horses and mules and ensuring a regularity of supply which animal transport had never been able to achieve.

However, it is the so-called 'Punctuation of Olmütz' that may be taken to mark the entry of the railway into power politics. The 'Punctuation' was an agreement between Austria and Prussia in 1850, in which Prussia temporarily capitulated to Austrian dominance rather than make war. The Prussian leadership had never been solidly in favour of fighting a war and there can be little doubt that its pacific leanings were considerably strengthened when a powerful Austrian army unexpectedly appeared on its Silesian frontier. This army, of 75,000 men and 8,000 horses, had been transported by rail.

It was remarked at the time that the Austrian troops took over three weeks to cover 150 miles; they could have moved just as fast on foot. Whether they would have arrived in the same condition is another matter. Armies habitually lost more men on the march than in battle, and although twenty-six days in a train may have been less comfortable than twenty-six days on the road the train trip would have been less wearying. Moreover, desertion from a train is harder than desertion from a column. In any case, the protracted journey time did not reflect the inadequacies of rail transport, but was a result of poor planning and of inexperience, unlikely to be repeated in future movements. Indeed, Vienna learned its lesson quickly. Six months after Olmütz it drew up a scheme of railway building in which strategic considerations were allowed to dominate, and at the same time it established a sensible routine for railborne troop movements. Thus in 1853 it was able to stage another mass troop movement, this time conducted with speed and precision, and without disturbing the railways' civilian traffic.

Thus it is Austria which deserves the credit for the first really convincing proof of the strategic implications of rail transport. However, this was less a radical departure than a step forward from previous developments. Troops had been carried by rail long before this, and discussions of strategic railways had, in some countries, actually preceded the introduction of railways. In the great controversies that raged in different countries over the possibility, and indeed utility, of building railways, the military implications were used as arguments by both sides. Proponents of railway-building pointed out that if railways were available to shift troops rapidly to any threatened sector of the frontier a country's defences could be enhanced. Opponents asserted that when an invader breached the frontier, his advance would be faster and more dangerous if he found a railway network at his disposal. This argument, which time and the experience of wars has tended to weaken, seemed very powerful at the time.

Because in the 1820s and 1830s the practicability of railways themselves was in doubt, their use as mass conveyors of armies was not always taken seriously, especially as those who advertised such a use had their own, highly commercial, reasons for using this argument. In Britain, France and the United States the economic justification for railways, and the initiative of promoters and investors, was quite sufficient to get the first lines started without any reference to military advantages. In Belgium and Germany, two other early entrants to the Railway Age, strategic arguments were put forward, but were neither necessary nor taken seriously. The first practical, if small, British demonstration of rail power between Manchester and Liverpool aroused less interest in Britain than it did abroad. Tsar Nicholas, whose Polish subjects were as unruly as King William's Irish subjects, was one of those who were impressed by the possibilities offered by railways in quelling internal disorders, and it is significant that a line from St Petersburg to Warsaw later became one of Nicholas's priorities.

In America, another kind of disorder was dealt with by railborne troops in 1831, when 100 soldiers were sent over the Baltimore & Ohio Railroad to arrest fifty railwaymen who were protesting at that Railroad's refusal to pay their wages. Seven years later Major-General Edmund Gaines of the US Army was investigating the possibilities of strategic railroads radiating from Kentucky and Tennessee—then central—to the frontiers of the USA. However, in his 1839 report to Congress Gaines seemed to feel that railroads should be regarded simply as aids to coast defence. But in 1846 there was a taste of the future when a regiment of Pennsylvania volunteers moving to New Orleans for the campaign against Mexico travelled part of the way by train.

Although in subsequent decades Prussia was to become a most diligent organizer of military railway transport, early German railway promoters had little success in persuading their governments that railways could be a good investment from the strategic point of view. Not only this, but the Prussian army leaders actively discouraged railway-building, believing that railways would threaten their system of defensive fortresses. A Westphalian entrepreneur and publicist, Friedrich Harkort, had in 1833 proposed a railway between the rivers Weser and Lippe. He followed this up with a publication advocating a railway between Minden and Cologne, in which he explicitly used military arguments, comparing the time taken on foot by Prussian soldiers between various centres with the time they would need to make the same journeys by rail. He went on to envisage a railway and a telegraph line extending along the Prussian side of the Rhine between Mainz and Wesel. With such an arrangement, he wrote, the French would no longer be able to make a crossing, because Prussian troops could be rushed to the spot before they had time to consolidate. However, neither the Prussian military nor the Prussian press accepted Harkort's ideas, preferring to make fun of him whenever they could not ignore him.

Prussian attitudes changed at the beginning of the 1840s. A military sceptic, Miller, wrote a pamphlet in 1836 in which he asserted that although steam railways might be of use for conveying supplies, the soldiers would reach their destination quicker if they marched. However, in 1841 the same writer published another work on the same subject, in which he was more optimistic; possibly his change of heart was a result of receiving more accurate data. Another very influential advocate was Carl Pönitz, whose book first appeared in 1842. Because he based his claim for the railway on very careful calculations, and because he succeeded in changing so many people's minds, his book is often regarded as the first really serious study of the military uses of railways. He himself seems to have taken this view, having a justified disdain for others who had made the same claims but never took the trouble to properly substantiate them:

'Hardly had Germany witnessed a few trains moving on its sections of railway in order to satisfy public curiosity or to train the operating staff, than several fine talkers were found who hastily and boldly pronounced on the military utility of these new communications. However, the data was inevitably super-ficial and hypothetical.... Timid souls shuddered at the thought of several hundred thousand bellicose Frenchmen, riding the new fire dragons, being able one fine spring morning to burst into the midst of our peaceful cantons.'

But after dismissing his predecessors, Pönitz had plenty of ammunition left for the army's conservatives:

'... The military sceptics looked at the new invention quite differently ... these gentlemen, in gaily diminishing the number and the power of locomotives and in reasoning more-over on quite arbitrary suppositions, did not fail to arrive at quite poor results and, basing themselves on these calculations, they could affirm that a corps of troops of all arms, sent to a distant destination, would reach it as quickly on foot as with railways and locomotives, and perhaps faster.... Many unprejudiced soldiers believed that this means of locomotion could serve at best for the transport of material, food, and forage, but never for military operations.'

Pönitz continued by indulging in what would become a best-loved dream of the armchair strategist, planning a network of strategic railways. However, he allowed reality to bring force to his dream, making thoughtful calculations for troop movements between a series of points. These calculations included rolling stock requirements, line capacity, and schedules. He envisaged what he called the 'double train', which was little different from the double-headed train of later decades. This standard double train was to have two locomotives and twenty-four cars, enough to move an 800-man battalion, with its carts and horses, 180 miles in one day and to continue the journey the following day. Thus an infantry brigade would be moved in six of these long trains, the general and his aides travelling in the first train because '... in view of the rapid movement it is easier to give orders towards the rear than towards the front'. He did not think cavalry should move by rail:

'The formidable noise of the machines and the strident and sharp steam whistles irritate the whole nervous system of horses and throw them into such anxiety that they often refuse all food for whole days and almost always arrive at their destination unfit for action.'

In exceptional cases, Pönitz thought, the horsemen with their saddles and baggage could move by train while the horses were led on foot. But he did not object to supply horses moving by rail. Indeed, over heavy gradients or during a locomotive shortage these horses could be ejected from their comfortable carriages and made to pull their trains.

The debates which followed the publication of Pönitz's book did not result in any great transformation of Prussian official opinion. Undoubtedly, however, some seeds were sown, for in 1848 the General Staff collected, and published, information about the equipment and capacity of German and foreign railways likely to be useful in a future war. Probably, though, it was the revolution of 1848 that did most to change the Prussian bureaucratic mind. Revolutionaries were not at all reluctant to use the new technologies, and the new railways vastly increased the speed with which they could spread their revolutionary ideas. As a result, some embattled regimes were occasionally prompted to use the railways to move troops as rapidly as possible to quell the uprisings. Already, during a prelude to the 1848 revolutions, the rebellious inhabitants of Kraków had been put in their place by a Prussian army, which had moved on to the city by rail. In the Italian revolts of 1848 the Austrians had made use of railways to shift their troops, while the revolutionaries of Venice blew up a section of the railway viaduct linking their city with the mainland.

Possibly one reason why the Prussians had not hurried to develop a strategy of railway-building was that their anticipated enemies, especially France, had made even less progress. In 1844 von Moltke, already a rising staff officer, contentedly wrote that despite everything Prussia had more railways than France. This was because in France there was a long gap between the first railways of the late 1820s and the definitive national railway plan of 1842. During these years the French discussed railways endlessly, but built very little. In the debates, centred on the National Assembly, military considerations were often emphasized, and some commentators saw a clear expression of military priorities in the French railway plan when it finally emerged. True, the projected lines, radiating from Paris, had a military neatness about them. True, too, that the projected lines would have enabled troops to be despatched from Paris to all the frontiers of France. But there was a tendency, from which modern historians have still not matured, to regard any railway which had strategic uses as a strategic railway. In the history of world railway-building there have been remarkably few railways built for purely strategic reasons. It was often the case that a route desirable for commercial reasons also happened to be the best for military purposes. Since the natural inclination of railways was to connect important centres, to thread passes, to cross rivers and to use the shortest possible routes, this was not surprising.

Russia has been especially maligned in this respect. Nineteenth-century British Russophobia ensured that almost any Russian railway project was thought of as being primarily intended for military purposes. The adoption in Russia of the 5 ft gauge instead of the 4 ft 8½ in gauge of Stephenson in use in the rest of Europe is still interpreted as a defensive move, intended to prevent foreign invaders arriving by train inside the Russian frontiers. Two decades after Tsar Nicholas I had chosen the wider gauge *The Times* of London could still assert in November 1866: '. . . the Russian Government, I am told, with a view to prevent an enemy advancing into the country by rail, have adopted a slightly narrower track than the one used on the rest of the Continent. . . .' This sentence, containing one error of fact and one of interpretation, would have been even less convincing if it had been written at the time to which it relates, because when Russia adopted the 5 ft gauge there was no standard gauge, even in England. Nicholas chose the gauge on the advice of an American engineer, who, in turn, was probably influenced by the 5 ft gauge used by many American railroads. Indeed, the wider gauge has often been a military hindrance to Russia; it is far easier for an invader to lay a narrowing rail on the existing track than it is for the Russians, in foreign territory, to lay a widening rail and to run wider rolling stock.

Given the military interests and character of Nicholas, it is hard to believe that he was oblivious of the strategic advantages of railways. But his empire was so vast, and the cost of railways so great, that he is unlikely to have foreseen a time when troops could be conveyed to any part of the frontiers by train. Railways as a means for the rapid movement of troops within the interior of the country was far more appealing; then, as later, the Russian administration feared its own people as much as foreign invaders. For Nicholas, one of the advantages promised by his first main line, between St Petersburg and Moscow, was that he would be enabled to station the Guards regiments in Moscow, where their upkeep was much cheaper than in St Petersburg. Moreover, added some commentators, the increased mobility of the army which would be gained by this and other railways would enable the army to be reduced in size, so that capital for railways might be obtained simply by a reduction of military expenses. However, the report by the American minister in St Petersburg that Nicholas had obtained the consent of his ministers for the building of the St Petersburg–Moscow Railway by promising to reduce the size of the army seems a very unlikely story.

In the 1840s there were some commentators who foresaw that when other countries, notably Germany and Austria, had built railways to their frontiers, the Russian government would be forced to do the same, simply as a military necessity. Nicholas's approval of the St Petersburg to Warsaw Railway was almost certainly influenced by strategic considerations even though the Russian army was then regarded as by far the world's most powerful. After the Crimean War in the 1850s had demonstrated the inadequacies both of the Russian army and of the Russian transport system, railway-building really got under way, with military considerations sometimes affecting the construction plans.

In the meantime the Russians had made good use of railway transport at critical times. Nicholas had approved the construction of the Warsaw–Vienna Railway, built to connect Warsaw with a line laid northwards by the Austrians, for purely commercial reasons, but in 1849 the railway was available when he wished to send help to the Austrian Emperor in his struggle against a Hungarian rebel army. Thanks to the timely arrival of the 30,000 Russian troops from Poland, the Hungarians were defeated.

The use which governments might make of railways for the movement of troops against internal dissidents had probably a greater appeal than the more purely strategic arguments. However, at a time when liberalism was becoming a strong ideological movement, this aspect was not necessarily conducive to railway-building. Liberals, and many of those with capital available for investment who liked to think of themselves as liberals, had doubts about building railways that might be used to strengthen the hands of authoritarian regimes. Advocates of railway construction sometimes had to choose their words very carefully. Cavour, for example, who later became an Italian statesman, took care to allay these fears when recommending more railways for Italy in 1845. Such railways would not be used by foreign powers to prevent the unification of the various Italian states, he wrote, because such a unification could '. . . only be the consequence of a remodelling of Europe, or of one of those great providential explosions in which the simple capacity to move troops rapidly by rail will have little importance'.

Thirteen years later a war in Italy demonstrated that, providential explosions or not, the railway could indeed affect the course of Italian history. The conflict between Austria on the one hand and France and Piedmont on the other was the first in which both sides relied on railways to transport their troops to the field of operations. The campaign began with the Piedmontese taking up positions to defend their capital, Turin, from the Austrian armies in northern Italy. Together with their Sardinian allies, they took great care to defend the railway from Genoa to Turin, for it was along that railway that the promised French supporting troops would travel. For the French, this was very much a prearranged war, so their troops moved with great speed to Italy; six days after the Austrian ultimatum the first French troops were disembarking in Genoa. During the three months of the war the French railways are said to have conveyed over 600,000 men and 130,000 horses. This figure probably incorporates a good deal of double-counting, but a quarter of a million men were conveyed either to the railheads of Marseilles and Toulon (for onward movement by sea) or to Aix, Culoz and Grenoble (for passage over the Alps). The biggest burden fell on the recently opened Paris–Lyons Railway, particularly in the last ten days of April, when 76,000 troops were conveyed to the south-eastern railheads; in pre-railway days regiments would have needed about two months for such a journey. The railways appeared to handle this traffic with great efficiency; the Paris–Lyons Railway did not even have to interrupt its civilian schedules. That the troops, after arriving so quickly in Italy, found themselves without adequate material support was hardly the fault of the railways. Evidently the military planners had failed to foresee that their troops might move faster than their supplies. This would not be the last time that the French railways coped effectively with military demands, only to find that their efforts had been undermined by lack of foresight on the part of the army.

But the shortcomings of French administration were slight compared with the chaos attending the Austrian troop movements. Despite their previous leading role in the exploitation of the new technology for military purposes, the Austrians failed badly in this, their first major test. This was only partly due to physical obstacles, such as the operating difficulties they faced on the line over the Semmering Pass, and the absence of a railway on the line of march between Innsbruck and Bolzano. More important was the almost complete lack of preparation for the campaign. Indeed, the one great lesson of this war—not always or everywhere absorbed—was that in the Railway Age troop and supply movements had to be planned well in advance; emergency timetables could not be drawn up, disseminated and understood at the last minute. At Vienna, which was a staging point for reinforcements sent not only from Austria proper but from the far-flung outposts of the Hapsburg empire in Poland, Bohemia and Hungary, a great shortage of rolling stock developed. One cause of this, again foreshadowing one of the big problems of later wars, was that the military authorities in Italy did not hasten to return empty rolling stock, preferring to keep it for their own real or imagined needs. At another staging point, Laibach (now Ljubljana in Yugoslavia), troop trains were delayed for hours and even days because their intended destination was unknown; the War Ministry's decisions were often made at the last possible moment, so that the instructions sent down the line arrived long after the train to which they referred had steamed into the station. The congestion caused by these delayed supply and troop trains also caused delays to other trains. On average, it was estimated that a unit took fourteen days to move from Vienna to the Lombardy battlefields. This was considerably longer than was technically possible, given proper organization, but it was four or five times faster than could have been achieved on foot.

This war was also notable for the tactical use made of railways. Using the railway, the Franco–Piedmontese forces were able to quickly and unexpectedly shift troops to an outflanking position, forcing the Austrians to evacuate Vercelli and thereby expose themselves to their major defeat at Magenta a few days later on 4 June 1859. Earlier, the first serious battle of the war at Monte-bello had resulted in an Austrian defeat, again partly due to the tactical use of railways by the Franco–Piedmontese forces. The correspondent of *The Times* dramatized this feature in words which were often quoted subsequently: '. . . from the heights of Montebello the Austrians beheld a novelty in the art of war. Train after train arrived by railway from Voghera, each train disgorging its hundreds of armed men and immediately hastening back for more.' Another commentator, lecturing to the Royal United Services Institution in London in 1861, spoke of injured men being 'brought swiftly back to the hospitals, still groaning in the first agony of their wounds' and of railway earthworks and bridges presenting 'features of importance equal or superior to the ordinary accidents of the ground, and the possession of which was hotly contested'.

The same lecturer claimed that this 'first employment of rail-ways in close connection with vast military operations would alone be enough to give a distinction to this campaign in military history'. All the same, military planners and readers of *The Times* might well have discerned a trace of exaggeration in these judge-ments. After all, although railways had been used on a large scale, the war would have probably ended in an Austrian defeat in any case; without the railways it would simply have taken longer. It was the American Civil War which would show that the acceleration of war which the railways brought could, in itself, be decisive.

Chapter 2

Railways in the American Civil War

By 1860 the military staffs of the great powers were well aware that railway transport would be important in future wars, but few realized just how decisive railways might be. It was the American Civil War which showed that the ability to run trains to the right place at the right time was not merely an advantage but a prerequisite of victory. When this conflict began it soon attracted hordes of military attachés and military observers; these were not slow to remark that this was very much a railway war, and their reports had a great influence on strategists everywhere. They might, however, have learned more if they had concentrated on the losing side rather than on the victorious Federals.

For it was the Confederates of the South who most depended on the railways. Outnumbered, lacking naval power and virtually surrounded, their only hope of victory lay in rapid concentrations of their entire strength against one part or other of the Federal army. For this they needed to take full advantage of their interior lines of communication; that is, of their railroads. At the same time they soon realized the importance of cutting the Northern lines of rail communication. Given the importance of railroads for the Southern cause, it is not surprising that the Confederates were the first to use a railway in order to win a battle, the first to introduce ambulance cars and rail-mounted guns, and the first to launch raids against the railroads of their opponent. What they did not do was impose a strict co-ordinating control over the numerous railway managements. The Federals, on the other hand, were much more successful in this, evolving a system that prevented railway managers acting selfishly and parochially, while at the same time keeping railway operation in the hands of railwaymen rather than military officers.

The railroads used by both sides were single track and, for the most part, of primitive construction. The American practice of building lines as cheaply as possible, relying on future traffic to finance eventual upgrading, meant that the lines of the early 1860s were laid on the ground with little drainage and minimal earthworks. The rails, spiked to cross-ties made of freshly cut wood, were of iron, except where so-called strap rail still survived. The latter consisted of timber rails on which an upper strip of iron was fastened. Locomotives were almost entirely of the 'American' type, with four driving wheels and a leading four-wheel truck to cope with the sharp curves. The wheels had tyres of iron, which, like the rails, were quick to wear out. All this meant that to remain viable a railroad had to be in a perpetual state of renewal as cross-ties rotted, rails broke or wore out, and locomotive and car tyres grew thinner. For the Northern railroads this was no great problem, but in the South there was little industrial capacity for railroad ironwork, nor any possibility of imports. Thus the Southern railroads were, literally, a depleting asset. By 1863, reported one Confederate colonel, the Virginia Central Railroad had cross-ties so rotten, and rails so ragged, that '. . . the ashpans of our Engines . . . press down upon the mud, like the plasterer does with his trowel'. In 1865 the Federals rehabilitated a captured Southern railroad, but General Porter observed that its '. . . undulations were so striking that a train moving along it looked in the distance like a fly crawling over a corrugated washboard'.

Both sides were handicapped, though not crippled, by the different gauges of their railroads. In the South two gauges predominated, 4 ft 8½ in and 5 ft. The Deep South favoured a gauge of 5 ft, whereas in Virginia, North Carolina and occasionally elsewhere, many important lines were 4 ft 8½ in. Since transhipment of freight and passengers between railroads was the rule, irrespective of gauge, this seemed to be a handicap only in emergencies, when the army wished to send troops long distances in through trains.

Re-gauging was rarely attempted. In the final months of the war, when the Confederates were trying to outpace Sherman, they were handicapped by the 4 ft 8½ in gauge of the North Carolina

Railroad. Seeking to change this to 5 ft, the gauge of neighbouring lines and of the bulk of available rolling stock, they were thwarted by the state governor, who categorically refused to allow any tampering with it.

The Federals also had their gauge problems; in particular, the railroad companies which provided the key trunk route from New York to Washington used 4 ft 8½ in in the north but 4 ft 10 in south of Philadelphia. However, it was not so much the gauge difference that prevented through running of trains as managerial attitudes (especially in the South) and the frequent absence of physical links between neighbouring railroads. Attitudes were those that might be expected from managements of small railroad companies built to serve local communities and which almost by accident linked up to form long routes. In the Southern states, for example, there were almost 10,000 miles of railroad, divided between 113 different companies. The main east to west route from Charleston on the Atlantic to Memphis on the Mississippi was 755 miles, divided between five companies, while the 1,215-mile link between Alexandria (near Washington) to the Gulf of Mexico near Mobile was the property of eleven railroads. Only at times of obvious crisis were the Southern military authorities able to run through trains.

Irrespective of gauge and managerial attitudes, through running on some routes was impossible because in several towns there was no rail connection between the terminals of neighbouring railroads. In Virginia alone Lynchburg, Petersburg and Richmond were three such cities. In Richmond, the military inconvenience caused by this absence was so great that temporary connecting tracks were eventually laid along the street. In Federal territory, Baltimore attained early notoriety in this respect. At the very beginning of the war troops from New England were despatched to defend Washington via the main line, which passed through Baltimore. There was a crude horse-drawn railroad through the city by which railroad cars could be conveyed between terminals, but the troops were ordered to march from one station to the other. As popular sentiment in Baltimore tended to favour the South, the riot which broke out as the troops marched through should not perhaps have been unexpected. The resulting bloodshed was an excellent reason, or pretext, for the city leaders to prevent a repetition simply by burning the railroad bridges. This not only satisfactorily isolated Baltimore but also cut off Washing-

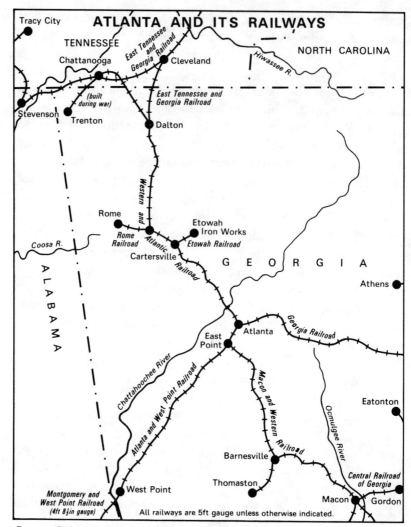

Source: *Robert C. Black*, Railroads of the Confederacy

ton from railborne reinforcement from the north until the bridges could be restored.

The failure of the Confederate government to impose central control over the railroad companies meant that the latter, except for occasional and ever-rarer bursts of patriotism, always put their own interests before those of the war effort. It is true that they had good cause to distrust the government. The latter paid its bills late, and made sudden demands which could be met only at a loss; its soldiers pilfered the railroads, removed wood intended for locomotive refuelling, broke up rolling stock and sometimes held up operations by mass drunkenness. Nevertheless, the selfishness of the Southern railroads was in clear contrast to the show of public spirit demonstrated by most of the Northern railroads.

Southern railroad managements regarded themselves as true patriots, but claimed that their first duty was to their shareholders. They would therefore, for example, oppose the interchange of rolling stock between railroads because they knew that their neighbours might never return any that had been borrowed. But at the same time they were unwilling to accept a fair pooling arrangement, just as they were unwilling to accept any central direction. Perhaps the railroad most determined to resist co-ordination, even in the direst crisis, was the only state-owned company, the Western & Atlantic. Owned and operated by the state of Georgia, Governor Brown of Georgia treated it as his favourite toy. In 1863, he decreed that the Confederate government should pay the railroad double what it paid other lines for the movement of troops and stores. The same year the Confederate General Bragg, whose supplies had been held up by the Railroad, threatened to seize it. Governor Brown responded by threatening to stop the Railroad's operations by sending all its employees home, and in the meantime informed the Confederate President that he would resist Bragg by force. The Governor had his way, and at the end of the year Bragg was still complaining that two of his battalions were stranded in Atlanta because the Railroad preferred to use its scarce rolling stock for ordinary passengers.

All the railroads were determined to squeeze as much money from the Confederate government as possible. At the very beginning of the war they had bravely declared that they would carry government traffic at half the normal tariff, but it was not long before they agreed to charge rates which in fact were higher than civilian fares. Nor were they unwilling to take advantage of the government's difficulties; when the massive and ultimately successful movement of troops leading to the battle of Chicka-mauga was under way between the eastern and the north-western fronts, one of the railways forming a link in the route—the Richmond and St Petersburg Railroad—immediately raised its charges. But although the companies supported each other in tariff policy, and in resisting government intervention, they fought each other on other matters. When Confederates brought back captured locomotives, or when locomotives were withdrawn from

Southern lines abandoned to the enemy, then the different companies used all kinds of threats and intrigues to obtain more than their fair share of the booty. With the increased traffic, locomotives in good condition were priceless.

Serious material shortages were felt in the South soon after the start of the war. At first, some at least of the railway managements took pride in their improvisations. The Seaboard & Roanoke Railroad, cut off by blockade both from its source of whale oil lubricants and from the Cincinnati bacon with which it fed its slave labour, built a pork factory which not only supplied its work force with food but also produced a substitute lubricant of pig fat. When iron fell into critically short supply, the Southern railroads clubbed together to send an agent through the blockade to seek supplies in England. But this mood did not last long. When rails became threadbare, when locomotives went out of service for lack of replacement tyres, each railroad looked after itself, hiding any iron supplies it might have and denouncing any hoarding on the part of its neighbours. Eventually a point was reached when the lines essential to the war could be kept in action only by lifting rails from secondary railways. Most railway managements agreed with this in general; but each resisted, by physical force sometimes, and by court action almost always, when one of its own branch lines was named as a potential 'iron mine'.

When things became worse it was not only branch lines but self-styled main lines whose rails were lifted and sent to the arterial lines. Such was the case with the Alabama & Florida Railroad, a company in which much local pride and capital had been invested but which was not considered essential for the Southern war effort. It had been built to help the port of Pensacola fight the competition of the neighbouring port of Mobile. After Pensacola had been occupied by the Northern forces the Confederate troops, under orders from Governor John Milton of Florida and the Engineering Bureau of the Confederate government, began to lift the rails of the portion still remaining in their hands. The Railroad's management was aghast; it had lost its terminus and its traffic but was determined not to lose its rails. Its president accused the port of Mobile of intrigue, and went to the Southern capital to confront the secretaries of War and of the Navy. He then scouted round the Southern states for caches of rail; he denounced several railroads for hoarding, at the same time making unwelcome suggestions about which railroads might be best sacrificed for the sake of their rails. All this, unusually, achieved nothing. The Confederate government desperately needed the rail and, for once, was not listening to appeals based on 'states' rights'. In the end only the meagre trackbed and rotten cross-ties of the Alabama & Florida were left. Even the locomotives were taken. Moreover, it was not until two years later that the Southern Congress voted to compensate the Railroad, so it received the agreed values of 1862 in the highly inflated currency of 1864.

Other sources of rail were lines abandoned on the advance of Northern forces. Usually there was insufficient foresight displayed to make this possible, but when the Northerners landed in Virginia's peninsula in 1862, the Southern generals did insist that not only the locomotives but also the rails of the local railroads should be evacuated. It would also have been possible to re-roll worn rails, but the few Southern ironworks were fully engaged in army and navy work. Old rail (as well as some hoards of new rail which the navy discovered) was thus used to make armour for the Confederate navy.

Although iron was the crucial material, the railroads were hampered by shortages in almost every aspect of their work All Southern locomotives burned wood, but most of the woodcutters had been drafted into the army, so it became difficult to guarantee supplies of wood at every refuelling point. Appeals to local landowners to rent out their slaves for these duties met only a half-hearted response, partly because many slaves already hired to the railroads had managed to escape. Boxcars used for troop transport had their sides cut away by the bayonets of soldiers who felt too warm under the southern sun. Worn wheels could not be replaced and this, like the rail shortage, meant a continual rise in the accident rate. Station buildings were neglected; a local paper described the station at Raleigh as a 'hog-wallow' with 'delicate women and children wading over their ankles'. The Virginia Central Railroad's new workshops could not be roofed because there was no slate.

Shortage of mechanics was also an early problem for the railroads. In the early days many railwaymen volunteered for military service in a fit of patriotism, and this loss of skilled men soon brought some railroads to the brink of collapse. Some companies appealed to the government and many men were sent back from the camps to their old jobs. But later, as the munition factories raised their pay rates to attract labour, many railway-men left to take jobs in industry. Thus the railway workshops, or at least that small proportion of them which had not been requisitioned for war production, found themselves short of labour even before they ran short of materials. As the war progressed, the army's conscription officers became increasingly aggressive in their attitude towards railwaymen, frequently drafting key workers into the army. Railroad managers began to deluge the capital with telegrams of complaint, sometimes asking directly for the release of specific employees and threatening serious consequences in case of refusal; '. . . compelled in self-defense to stop supplies for Charlotte Q.M. and Naval post . . .' telegraphed one railroad president. Such appeals were usually heeded, but in 1863 the railroads were limited in the number of employees of military age that they could retain, and each exempted man was properly registered. This measure was one reason for the shortage of unskilled labour on the railroads. For a time each railroad tried in one way or another to steal its neigh-bours' men, but this could be no solution to the total problem. Since Negroes were not conscripted, railroads began to advertise for slave labour, but slave-owners were unwilling either to rent or sell their labour forces. Some companies, however, by offering sufficiently high prices, did purchase useful numbers of black workers.

As the first conflict in which railways played a key part, the Civil War witnessed the emergence of problems which would reappear in later wars. Among these was the question of authority and control—who should direct railway operations in the war zones? Both the North and the South soon learned that neither control by army officers nor control by private railway manage-ments could work. In the North the problem was solved by a strictly imposed compromise. In the South nothing could be strictly imposed, and every compromise failed accordingly. Because the Confederates' quarrel with the North centred around their demand for freedom from interference from Washing-ton, they were psychologically incapable of accepting that their railroads should be subject to interference from their own government.

Thus in the South there was a continued animosity between railroad administrators and the local army officers, who tried to impose their own priorities. Railwaymen were sometimes slow to see the urgency of military transportation needs, but they had the excuse that officers presented every demand in terms of special urgency. Army officers, including the quartermasters who were appointed to supervise the army's supply and transportation arrangements, were all too frequently ignorant of how delicately interlocked railway operations were, and consequently brought trains to a standstill amid chaos which might take days to sort out.

Military complaints about railway operators' inefficiency or apparent bloody-mindedness were often justified. But even more justified and common were the railwaymen's complaints about military high-handedness. A typical misdemeanour of military officers, which would be repeated in subsequent wars elsewhere, was the detention of scarce freight cars. The shortage of rolling stock was almost as crippling in the South as the shortage of rails and locomotives, but could in theory be alleviated by using the cars more intensively. In effect this meant faster loading, unloading and return of empties. But despite exhortations from the railroad managements, local military officers held on to their cars. Often it was a case of caution. Every local commander wanted to safeguard himself against future eventualities; that was the mark of a successful officer. But when this insurance entailed the withholding of lines of empty boxcars in case of need, what was good for one sector of the front could be disastrous for the transportation system as a whole. Less forgivable, but equally damaging, was the use of boxcars by the army commissary departments as warehouses. It was so much easier to keep supplies in the boxcars in which they arrived rather than transfer them to storehouses, which in many cases had to be specially built. Early in the war the nature of the problem could easily be discerned. When the government wished to send a consignment of flour to the front, the Virginia Central Railroad pointed out that it had only two empty cars available, as all the rest were being held by government or military agents. Again, in 1862, when the Confederates wanted to move troops quickly from east Virginia to the Shenandoah Valley to exploit the victories of Stonewall Jackson, the two railroads involved had no rolling stock available; it had all been sent westwards to pick up prisoners of war, and a military quartermaster who was supervising transportation at Lynchburg refused to send it back. The necessary equipment was hastily borrowed from another company, but the delay and confusion meant that the Confederates' plans had to be changed.

The practice of military officers demanding special trains at short notice, thereby disrupting the schedules of all other trains on the line, was a constant source of friction. Quite early in the war the management of the East Tennessee & Virginia Railroad threatened to cease all operations if this interference did not cease. Such threats—repeated by different railroads throughout the war—usually had no more than a temporary and local effect. Another common practice, even more destructive of railway efficiency, was the commandeering of trains by the military. A notorious example of this occurred during the evacuation of Atlanta, when the Confederate commander, justifiably irritated by a railroad's preference for serving civilians rather than troops, commandeered a passenger train and sent it off loaded with his wounded. He did not notify the railroad's management, with the result that there was a head-on collision with a northbound supply train. Not only were there thirty deaths because of this, but the single-track line—by then Atlanta's only link with the Confederate hinterland—was blocked for several hours and two locomotives and much rolling stock were lost.

Another example of military high-handedness occurred in 1864, when a corps had to be swiftly moved just sixty miles to reinforce Breckinridge after his victory at New Market. The troops were to detrain at Lynchburg, but it was to Lynchburg that all rolling stock had been despatched for safety earlier. Thus the empty stock had to be brought first to the entraining point at Charlottesville. This was not too difficult, despite the poor physical condition in which the Southern lines found themselves in 1864. But the commander of the reinforcing troops refused to allow his men to be sent off in batches, as each train of empties arrived. He insisted that not one of his soldiers would move until all the necessary trains had been assembled to his satisfaction, throwing the railroad's operations into confusion and ensuring that his troops arrived too late to achieve the anticipated crushing victory over the Northern forces.

At each main station railwaymen had to cope not only with the usual difficulties of wartime and shortages, but with a horde of military quartermasters and government agents whose business it was to bully the stationmaster into giving priority to those shipments in which they were interested. In these situations it was usually the military who got their way. This often meant that local military needs, often of quite imaginary urgency, took priority over movements which were essential for the Confederate economy as a whole. The railroads themselves sometimes found that their most essential service trains, carrying repair materials, lubricants and sometimes even locomotive fuel, were held up for days at stations *en route* because of the demands of a local quarter-master.

Sometimes, though, the military authorities seemed to have some justification for intervention, especially where inessential civilian traffic was accepted by the railroads at times when the front-line troops were short of ammunition and supplies. The shortages in the civilian economy meant that it was possible for shady characters to make immense profits by supplying needy areas with scarce goods, and such men did not hesitate to bribe railwaymen to expedite their shipments. Indeed, if bribes were not offered they might be demanded by the railwaymen. In 1862, General Pemberton, unable to build up food stocks for his troops, ordered the Mobile & Ohio Railroad to refuse civilian shipments of bacon and corn until his own troops were sufficiently supplied. This order was greatly resented by the local citizenry, which was ultra-patriotic in everything except self-sacrifice. When a local merchant packed his bacon into a coffin purporting to carry the body of a fallen Confederate soldier and sent it by train into Mobile, the Mobile newspaper reported his exploit with great enthusiasm and admiration.

The military authorities certainly had good cause to distrust the railwaymen. In 1862 the conductor of a freight train refused to pick up four carloads of urgently needed ammunition. Complaints reached the Secretary of War, who thereupon discovered that his Quartermaster-General had no control over the railroads; he could make himself a nuisance, threaten force even, but could be outmanoeuvred by the railroads in the courts and among the politicians. But the principal complaint throughout the war was not so much of dull unco-operativeness as of general inefficiency. For much of this the railroads could not be blamed. The dangerous state of the track made reductions of average speed essential, so that by the final year of the war a passenger train which averaged more than 10 miles per hour was exceptional. But when generals found that their troops were taking three days to cover less than a hundred miles they had every reason to suspect that it was not simply material shortages which were to blame. And irrespective of who was to blame, transport failures were demoralizing to everybody concerned, to generals whose strategy was confounded by the delayed arrival of rein- forcements and supplies, to troops who arrived on the battlefield after sitting in cramped trains for days on end, and to shippers of urgent freight, who made every effort to send off their products promptly only to see them lying in railway yards awaiting ship- ment. In 1862 one of the South's few metalworks, a rolling mill in Atlanta, worked heroic hours of overtime making armour plate for an ironclad being prepared for the defence of New Orleans, but because of railroad delays the plate arrived just as New Orleans was being abandoned.

After the war was over and the unsuccessful generals began to write their memoirs, it was the railroads which were all too often blamed for the South's military failures. This was unfair, though not unexpected. On a number of occasions the railroads enabled the generals to concentrate faster than their opponents and to win victories which were never energetically followed up. All the same, there is little doubt that the railroads gave priority to the needs of their own civilian customers except at times of grave crisis. This was a result of the structure of the railroad industry, with its multiplicity of very small companies all built to serve the needs of their own localities.

Throughout the war there were attempts to solve the problem of co-ordination. In the first months, the Confederate President appointed an assistant quartermaster to take charge of all rail transport in Virginia. The man was capable and the idea was good, but the President, sensitive to Southern susceptibilities, omitted to give him any powers. Any results had to be achieved by persuasion, which took a long time and was usually unsuccessful. In the second year of the war this weakness was sufficiently recognized for the Southern House of Representatives to con- sider a bill which would introduce a high-ranking military chief of transportation, a former railroadman, with other railroad operators given military ranks to serve as his subordinates. An independent agency would supervise the interchange of rolling stock between railroads, and through inter-railway schedules would be introduced for government traffic. This was exactly what the situation demanded, but it never succeeded in gaining the approval of Congress; too many local interests resented out- side interference in their business. As the war progressed, and transport went from bad to worse, new schemes were introduced, including a supervisory Railroad Bureau. But it was only in February 1865, when the war was virtually lost, that Congress granted real and overriding powers to the government for the regulation of railroad transport.

However, the shortcomings of the Confederate railroads were less important than the contribution which they made to the Southern cause. Indeed, without the railroads the Confederates would have been defeated years earlier. Having fewer resources, it was only their ability to concentrate their forces at strategic points which enabled them to hold off the Northerners for so long. Financially, the war had started quite well for the railroads. There was a surge of passenger traffic because the troop trains were additional to, not a replacement of, normal passenger trains. Civilian passenger traffic in fact increased, especially when families began to visit their kinsmen in the army, and this persisted even when ticket office queues, packed waiting rooms and unpleasantly crowded, slow and unreliable trains might have acted as a deterrent. On several of the important lines passenger traffic doubled during the first two years. In the first weeks of the war soldiers were not required to buy tickets, the railroads merely sending in their troop-carrying bills to the government. However, it was not long before civilian passengers discovered they could obtain a free ride merely by persuading train conductors that they were recruits. General Lee seems to have been the first to take counter-measures, declaring that the government would henceforth pay only those bills which were accompanied by transport vouchers collected from the soldiers.

The first full-scale battle of the war, and the first Confederate victory, was also the first battlefield victory achieved through the use of rail power. The First Battle of Bull Run began as a Northern attack on part of the Confederate army encamped close to Manassas Junction, south-west of Washington. The Confederate force was much the smaller, but as the Northern attack had been anticipated days in advance, orders had already been sent to General Johnston, commanding 11,000 troops, to move eastwards as reinforcement. Johnston's troops believed their movement was a retreat, and marched dispiritedly and slowly, so

(overleaf) *Desolation at Manassas Junction in March 1862. This station, south of Washington, was closely involved in the Confederate victories at the first and second battles of Bull Run*

the General asked for help from the nearby Manassas Gap Railroad. When his troops reached Piedmont Station soon after dawn they found trains awaiting them. However, the resources of this small railroad were limited. When the troop trains departed, only part of Johnston's force had been accommodated. The remaining troops had to wait until the trains had reached their destination and been returned empty. Not only this, but when the trains did finally return at midnight their enginemen vanished, saying that they had already worked twenty-four hours and that no wheel would turn until they had had a good night's sleep. The next morning, fuming officers finally got their men aboard and the trains left. But even the late arrivals were able to take part in the final stages of the battle, a battle which could not have been won without the railway.

After Bull Run, the railroads of both sides took part in removing the wounded to hospitals in the rear. Quite unprepared for this work, they usually provided freight cars with straw on the floors to cushion the blows transmitted from the virtually unsprung wheels as they hit successive rail joints. The agonies which the men suffered, and the unnecessary deaths which resulted, persuaded several railroads to fit out special ambulance cars. First to do this was the Confederate Wilmington & Weldon Railroad, which fitted out a twenty-patient ambulance car within a week of the battle. Later in the war the railroads of both sides operated complete ambulance trains, while the Federals introduced the concept of the self-contained hospital train on their captured Orange & Alexandria Railroad. Such hospital trains had ward cars for the patients, and separate cars for the medical staff, medical equipment and kitchens. When General Sherman captured Atlanta he was served by three such trains, plying between Louisville and Atlanta, and although they passed through Southern territory they were attacked neither by Confederate cavalry nor by saboteurs. Sherman's hospital trains could carry up to 200 patients and were the forerunners of the hospital trains used by the great powers in later conflicts.

The South was also first to employ the rail-mounted gun. General Lee, who always had a sound appreciation of how railways might be used in war, seems to have been the originator of this idea, which was employed effectively at the Battle of Savage Station in June 1862. Constructed for him by the Confederate navy, it consisted of a flatcar carrying a 32-pounder gun and

Predecessor of the armoured train: the Confederates' rail-mounted 32-pounder gun at Petersburg, Virginia. General Robert E. Lee is credited with this idea, which was used at the Battle of Savage Station

protected by iron plates. It was clearly a weapon of limited use, since it was confined to the railway line, but it was a means of bringing heavy firepower rapidly into action. However, this single vehicle was not a true armoured train. The latter seems to have been introduced by the Federals. The Baldwin Locomotive Works built a railway battery for the Northern army which was similar in concept to Lee's railway gun and the Federals subsequently operated trains of several similar vehicles. On the Baltimore & Ohio Railroad, which was most subject to attack, a six-car armoured train was used as a means of protecting and reconnoitring the railroad. However, the career of this train came to an end when its locomotive boiler was penetrated by a Confederate shell.

The first of the large-scale Confederate troop concentrations, the movement of 40,000 men northwards and westwards to

Corinth in north-eastern Mississippi in 1862, took place over a small number of comparatively large railroads. It was not therefore shortage of rolling stock which was the main obstacle but lack of organization and low morale. By no means did all of the railwaymen favour the Southern cause, and accusations that some locomotive men actually obstructed the movements probably had some foundation. But even loyal employees were resentful, because they had not received their regular pay for weeks or because Confederate troops had commandeered their living quarters. Troop trains were held up for hours because fuelling points were unmanned and the troops sometimes had to disembark to gather wood. All the same, most of the troops and most of their supplies did get through, and it was no fault of the Southern railroads that the resulting Battle of Shiloh was lost.

An immediate result of this defeat was that the railroads had to withdraw the men they had so laboriously brought to the front. And this time there were thousands of wounded among them. The evacuation of Corinth was well planned. The difficulty was that the railroads were unable to provide enough empty cars to make the plan realizable. The men had so much personal baggage that the stations were impossibly congested until General Bragg ordered that all trunks should be burned; '. . . great is the consternation . . .' he commented when reporting the response to this decision. Seven trains with military stores which were destined for the west rather than the south were, for some unaccountable reason, held back in Corinth and not released until after the railroad bridges had been burned by the rearguards. However, the trains sent south got through. In the final hours a train was run noisily forwards and quietly backwards to mislead Northern scouts into believing that trainloads of reinforcements were arriving.

After the Northern capture of Corinth the direct west to east railway through Corinth to Chattanooga was lost to the Confederates, and Federal forces advanced towards the city. General Bragg decided he could turn the tables by reinforcing his Chattanooga forces before the Northerners arrived to besiege the city. This meant moving troops from the north-eastern corner of Mississippi southwards down the Mobile & Ohio Railroad to Mobile, ferrying them across Mobile Bay, and then sending them over several railroads, including one standard-gauge line, to Atlanta, from where they would be in striking distance of Chattanooga. A trial move of one division was very successful, and this was followed by the transfer of the entire army of the Mississippi.

The move was well organized. It was decided that all horse units would go overland by the short and direct route. The whole of the infantry, however, was routed over the railroads. The six participating railroads were warned well in advance of what was expected of them, and the troops were sent division by division over a period of days from the entraining station at Tupelo. Every man took with him a week's rations, which made it unnecessary for trains to be delayed by foraging parties. More-over, at three cities *en route* the army supply departments organized extra food supplies on the station platforms. Discipline was emphasized at junction points, so there could be no cases of mass drunkenness delaying the departure of trains. The move, which transported about 25,000 men over more than 750 miles of rail-road, was virtually completed in ten days, and the strategic position was thereby transformed.

However, as was so often the case, the Confederate generals did not make full use of their opportunities, and this rail transfer did not bring the great victory it could have done. In September 1863 General Bragg evacuated Chattanooga, fearing an out-flanking movement, and called for reinforcements from the east. From Virginia and the Carolinas troops were despatched in a fairly well organized move over railroads which were already overloaded and physically worn out. As far as Atlanta two single-track routes were available, and although one was seventy miles longer than the other its use was well advised, for congestion would have been unmanageable otherwise. Even with two routes, the steady stream of troop trains towards the west dis-rupted all other railroad movements. Trains moving in the opposite direction had to be side-tracked so often that they were soon running up to twelve hours late. Most troops were carried in four days over the 705 miles from the Northern capital of Rich-mond to Atlanta, where the majority were kept for final battle preparations and then transported up the Western & Atlanta Railroad towards the expected battlefield. Unfortunately General Bragg got himself entangled in the Battle of Chickamauga before all the new troops arrived. Only about 6,000 of the 12,000 men detrained in time to fight, and many of these were disgorged from the trains almost on the battlefield itself. Nevertheless it was a famous victory, and demonstrated the railway's potential.

In the final year of the war the railroads still in Confederate hands were capable of troop movements, but only just. Added to the deteriorating state of the equipment and the lack of experienced labour was the destruction caused by raiding parties of Northern cavalry. Although repair gangs had been formed, often of Negroes, these needed days or weeks to repair burned bridges. In May 1864, when reinforcements were urgently needed in

Near Brandy Station on the Confederates' Orange & Alexandria Railroad in 1864. A construction gang restores the track after the derailment of the locomotive Government *and its train*

northern Virginia, it took four days to move troops over the 433 miles separating Charleston from Petersburg. In March 1865, when the Confederates tried to concentrate forces to block Sherman's advance in North Carolina, their railroads could no longer perform miracles and Sherman suffered only a minor hindrance. A few weeks later the railroads carried out their last major evacuation as the Confederate government abandoned its capital at Richmond and fled over the tracks of the threadbare Richmond & Danville Railroad. As usual, the rearguard destroyed railway bridges, buildings and all the locomotives which could not be moved. In early April General Lee's hungry and

weary men surrendered near Appomattox Station, having spent their last hours trying to make contact with four supply trains that the South Side Railroad had organized.

The Federals, by contrast, had been able to maintain and even improve their railroads during the war. Moreover, they had fewer inhibitions about centralized control and co-ordination. What was obviously the lifeline of the Federal army protecting Washington, the Philadelphia, Wilmington & Baltimore Railroad, was taken over by the government on the eve of the war. Subsequently the government took over lines only very rarely, for it could exercise control in other ways. An 1862 Act of Congress, enabling it to take over such railroads as it wished, was itself a persuasive weapon against recalcitrant managements. In the discussion on this bill the Chairman of the Committee on Military Affairs evidently understood what was vital: 'The object is . . . to move large masses of men without the knowledge or consent of anybody, without negotiating with railway directors as to how many men are to be moved, or where they are to be moved, or what rolling stock is wanted . . . to concentrate the rolling stock of a large number of railways, if it shall be necessary, on one railway line. . . .'

The United States Military Railroads was the organization which, among other things, operated lines taken over or built by the government. It began with two lines from Alexandria (near Washington) built to supply troops stationed nine and eleven miles distant. These two lines were not, however, the world's first military railways; apart from the Balaclava Railway of the Crimean War, the Confederates had already in 1861–62 built their Manassas–Centreville line to supply a winter encampment of their own. In the later years of the war the USMR was kept busy operating lines captured from the Confederates. In 1862 the Secretary of War appointed the Scotsman Daniel C. McCallum, manager of the Erie Railroad, as Director of Military Railroads. Beneath McCallum was a hierarchy of local railroad operators, railwaymen who, like McCallum, had been granted a military rank sufficiently high to ensure that they could get done what needed to be done.

Although the Federals, having better river and sea routes, made less use of railway troop movements than did their opponents, some notable transfers were made. After the defeat at Chickamauga, reinforcements of over 20,000 men were sent by train from the Army of the Potomac, taking only a week to cover 1,200 miles. Interestingly, the General-in-Chief of the army had protested that this could not be done, but had been overruled by the Secretary of War, primed by McCallum. This move probably saved the North from a serious situation, and turned the tide in its favour in Tennessee.

In addition to the advantage of better organization and real executive power, McCallum faced material difficulties that may have seemed daunting at times but were on nothing like the scale of those experienced in the South. True, there was an iron shortage, and some secondary lines had to be lifted to provide rails. Some railway workshops were largely devoted to war production. High-calibre railroadmen were reluctant to accept positions on the lines taken over by the government because service with the private companies seemed to offer more than service with the United States Military Railroads. But on the whole railroad operations in the north were never badly affected by shortages, and there were plenty of materials available for reconstruction and for the conversion of several stretches of 5 ft gauge line to the standard 4 ft 8½ in gauge.

Despite the government's directives, the railroads were not immune to interference from military commanders, especially during the first year of war. In Virginia, General Pope ignored Haupt, the local chief of transportation, who went home in disgust. Within ten days, however, the General's men had reduced the railroad first to chaos and then to immobility and Haupt was sent back with enhanced powers. But Pope never learned how to make proper use of his railroads, and this was one cause of his military failures. A typical example of his attitude was his order to Haupt to send all rolling stock to sidings near his army '. . . so that in case of necessity I can carry off all the baggage and material of the army at the shortest notice'. Haupt was soon in trouble with another general when he refused to disorganize his schedule in order to move 10,000 men a mere eighteen miles. Threatened with arrest, and faced with the appropriation of his railroad by determined regular officers, he appealed to higher authority, which thereupon threatened to arrest the general.

At a lesser but nevertheless fundamental level, the Northern railroads were hindered just as much as the Southern by the failure of the army to load and unload scarce freight cars promptly, and by the predilection of officers to use the railroads to carry all kinds of private goods and baggage. But by the end of 1862, with the faithful backing of the Secretary of War, McCallum had more or less eliminated these problems. On one occasion an assistant secretary of war signalled the divisional chief of railroads: 'Be patient as possible with the Generals. Some of them will trouble you more than they will the enemy.' The crucial move came in November 1862, when the Secretary of War issued an order which not only threatened with punishment any officer who delayed freight cars, but also concluded: 'No officer, whatever may be his rank, will interfere with the running of the cars, as directed by the superintendent of the road. Any one who so interferes will be dismissed from the service. . . .'

The division of responsibility between railroad operators and military officers was solved surprisingly well by the Federals, given the lack of previous experience. The tendency of soldiers to try to direct the operations of their local railways was very strong, and needed equally strong and clear directives to keep it in check. In subsequent decades some armies, like the Prussian, noted the American experience, and solved the problem. Others, like the French until the 1880s and the Russians until the Second World War, did not and paid highly for the omission. The inability of military men to see how delicately a railway organizes its movements, and how interference with the running of just one train can affect many other trains over hundreds of miles and for several days, made it imperative that experienced railwaymen should have the last word. It was no use for generals to threaten to shoot stationmasters who would not provide the trains they demanded. Edwin Pratt, in his study of military railways, stated the case clearly: '. . . a railway must be regarded as a delicate piece of transportation machinery which can easily be thrown out of order, and is capable of being worked only by railwaymen as skilled in the knowledge of its mechanism, and as experienced in the details of its complicated operation, as military officers themselves are assumed to be in the technicalities of their own particular duties. The Chief Goods Manager of a leading line of railway who offered to take the place of a General at the seat of war would arouse much mirth in the Army at his own expense. It is, nevertheless, quite conceivable that the General would himself not be a complete success as a Chief Goods Manager. . . .'

Another problem faced by Northern railroads were the Confederate raids made on them right from the very first weeks of the war. As a means of slowing down the expected Northern advance this was a sound tactic, for the Northern generals, in the aftermath of such raids, would be more reluctant than ever to leave the security of their supply bases. The Baltimore & Ohio Railroad suffered most; being virtually in No Man's Land, and forming the key link between Washington and the Federal forces in the west, it was a natural target for the Confederates. Its Martinsburg yards and workshops were captured and wrecked more than once, its bridges were burned, and its rolling stock wrecked. As the age of total war was only just dawning, freight trains were sometimes allowed to pass through zones occupied by the Confederates; seeking to win the hearts and minds of the Marylanders the Confederates tried to placate local commercial interests. Colonel Jackson, later General Stonewall Jackson, took advantage of this situation to decimate the Railroad's locomotive stock; earlier than most others, Jackson had realized that locomotive power in this war might become as important as firepower. He informed the local railroad management that its trains kept his troops awake at night, and it was arranged that trains should enter the Confederate zone only between 11 am and 1 pm. Having made this arrangement, Jackson realized he had laid a magnificent trap; almost all the rolling stock of the Company's eastern region was massed each day between those hours in the Confederate zone. By blocking all departures at midday, Jackson captured no fewer than fifty-six locomotives and 350 freight cars. He then destroyed bridges and track so that it would be weeks before they could be extricated, and departed. On a later raid he rediscovered the locomotives and cars and, the war having become more destructive and a little less respectful of private property, decided to make a bonfire of them. A few days later, realizing that locomotives were not so easily destroyed, he returned to the scene of what Northerners were already describing as his crime. He brought with him railway mechanics, who selected the best dozen or so of the locomotives. These were then taken over the highway, hauled by forty-horse teams, to the South, where they were used by the Southern railroads. Jackson meantime continued to wreck as much as he could of the property which could not be carried away, throwing some locomotives into the river, attacking others with sledgehammers, setting fire to bridges and coal trains. In all, the B & O lost sixty-seven of its precious locomotives and was closed for months between Baltimore and Wheeling.

In April 1862, the Confederates made a very destructive raid on the line which had previously connected Washington, the Federal capital, with their own capital at Richmond. Bridges were burned, rail removed and taken south, and cross-ties burned, with the result that the line could not be used for an intended concentration of Northern troops. It was this dire situation which prompted the Northern Secretary of War to call in the railway engineer Haupt to take charge of the Virginia railroads and supervise restoration. Haupt soon rebuilt the bridges, using trestle and crib constructions fashioned from wood cut and carpentered at the lineside. President Lincoln, who observed a 400-foot, four-storey bridge built by Haupt in a few days, was evidently impressed: '. . . that man Haupt has built a bridge across Potomac Creek . . . over which loaded trains are running every hour, and, upon my word, gentlemen, there is nothing in it but beanpoles and cornstalks.'

It was the difficulties which Haupt experienced on this first assignment which prompted him to persuade the army to form a special construction force. Hitherto ordinary soldiers had been drafted to help with railway reconstruction; these men not only lacked skill and experience, but were also often resentful, feeling that labouring work was unsoldierly. Haupt's early construction corps was simply a collection of soldiers who were permanently detailed for railroad reconstruction, and were provided with proper tools for the job. Later he established stocks of repair materials at strategic points, and repair trains were kept in reserve. By adding standard sixty-foot bridge spans to his stock, he was able to replace destroyed bridges at short notice. (The Confederates also provided themselves with spare spans, but on a smaller scale.) In 1862, Haupt was eventually appointed Chief of Construction and Transportation in Virginia, and went on to become a Brigadier-General, a rank which enabled him to wield the necessary authority when ordinary army officers tried to interfere in railroad affairs.

Haupt's work in 1862 led to the development of the larger Construction Corps established by McCallum which, among other things, assured Sherman of supplies on his long march to Atlanta in 1864. McCallum's Corps reached 10,000 men at one stage. It was divided into self-contained divisions, each with its allotted number of technical men, among whom the tracklayers and bridge-builders were the most important. Although not concerned with railway operation, these divisions can be regarded as forerunners of railway battalions in other armies; they not only restored damaged railways but brought existing lines up to the standards required to cope with heavy war traffic. In particular, they put in new sidings and loops on the single-track lines, in order to increase the number of trains which could be passed, and they improved and added locomotive watering and fuelling points.

One of the greatest of the Confederate railroad raids was staged by General Morgan and his cavalry at Christmas in 1862. The chosen victim was the Louisville & Nashville Railroad, the line which would be needed by Federal forces moving to attack Georgia from the Louisville direction. So vital was this line that the Federals had taken great pains to protect it from raiders. Bridges had stockades at each end, encampments of several hundred men were distributed along the line, and guardposts had been erected at key points. Nevertheless, mainly by virtue of surprise, Morgan's men overpowered one stronghold after another, destroying bridges and uprooting track.

The destruction of railroads became more sophisticated as the war went on. In the early stages of the war, with the wooden trestle bridge being the standard construction, fire seemed by far the easiest method of destruction. Brushwood would be piled around the bases of the supports, petroleum or tar would be poured as liberally as supplies permitted over the whole structure, and the brushwood ignited. This did not always work; in wet weather, when the raiders worked too hurriedly, sufficient damage was not always done. It was also a somewhat time-consuming method, which was a hindrance for raiders, whose work could not be accomplished without the element of speed and surprise. Later in the war, therefore, it became common practice to destroy bridges by inserting gunpowder 'torpedoes' into holes bored in the main timbers of the bridges. Fire remained, however, the chosen means of destroying rolling stock. Locomotives were also sometimes burned, although the effects were not lasting unless sledgehammers were also skilfully applied to sensitive parts such as the valve gear. The best way of destroying loco-motives was an artillery shot through the boiler, but it was only rarely possible to bring up a gun for this job. An alternative was to light a hot fire in the firebox, after emptying the boiler; this would melt the firetubes and necessitate laborious repair. As for rails, the early Confederate raids on the B & O sometimes successfully lifted the rails and despatched them for use on the Southern lines. However, there was rarely time or resources available for this solution to be adopted. It was soon discovered that tearing the rails from their cross-ties caused merely a temporary inconvenience to the enemy. Making a bonfire of cross-ties and then placing rails on top was the next step, but even this did not prevent the rails being relaid. So it became the practice to take the hot rails to be bent round trees by teams of soldiers. Even this was not enough, according to General Slocum, who had great experience in this field: 'Unless closely watched, soldiers will content themselves with simply bending the rails around trees. This should never be permitted. A rail which is simply bent can easily be restored to its original shape. No rail should be regarded as properly treated till it has assumed the shape of a doughnut; it must not only be bent but twisted.'

The same officer calculated that with a properly organized and disciplined force, 1,000 troops could utterly destroy five miles of

After a cavalry raid; for the cavalry, rendering rails unusable was often too time-consuming, but the trackwork shown in this picture would not be easily restored

track per day. Rain, of course, could be a great hindrance, as was shown during the great Federal raid on the Western & Atlantic Railroad. This, which became better known as Andrews' Raid or The Great Locomotive Chase, aimed to destroy the Confederate rail link between Chattanooga and Atlanta in April 1862. It began when Captain J. J. Andrews, a Union officer, and nineteen Federal soldiers, dressed as civilians and posing as refugees, boarded the northbound mixed train twenty miles from Atlanta. This train, headed by the freight locomotive *General*, made the customary breakfast stop at Big Shanty, during which the raiders uncoupled the passenger cars and took the locomotive and freight cars forward. The train's conductor, W. A. Fuller, who, because of his tenacity, was destined to become something of a folk hero, at first thought that deserters from a nearby army camp had made off with his train and would soon abandon it. But he was not content to let the matter take its course. To the amusement of the onlookers, he ran off in pursuit. On reaching the next station, he was told that the men aboard the train had taken down telegraph wires and had loaded track tools. It seems that at this point Fuller began to suspect that he was dealing with saboteurs. Together with two locomotive men, who had also run up the line, Fuller set off in pursuit aboard a hand-propelled track car. They had to manhandle their car over a short section where Andrews and his men had wrecked the track, but soon reached Etowah, where they commandeered an old yard locomotive. By this time they had been joined by a posse of alarmed citizens, and had acquired firearms. At Etowah, six Confederate soldiers joined the party, which set off at high speed aboard the locomotive, running tender first.

Meanwhile, Andrews had persuaded a railroad agent that he was a Confederate officer taking three urgent carloads of ammunition to the Southern forces. Southbound freights were side-tracked to allow his passage and he proceeded northwards, occasionally stopping to damage the track behind him. When Fuller and his men reached a stretch of torn track, they left their locomotive and, after running a couple of miles, met a southbound freight, hauled by the *Texas*. Its driver agreed to reverse, and the freight cars were pushed backwards until they could be dropped in a siding. Then the *Texas*, with Fuller and a somewhat depleted body of pursuers, hurried tender first after the raiders. The latter had dropped cross-ties on the track, but these presented no great obstacle. Towards the end of the chase, when the raiders first caught sight of the *Texas*, they uncoupled a freight car as they made off. The *Texas* hit the car at reduced speed and both remained on the track. The pursuit continued. A second freight car was soon encountered, but was similarly dealt with, and at a convenient siding the two cars were dropped. Finally the raiders uncoupled their last freight car, first setting it on fire. The *Texas* treated this obstacle more gently, catching it at very slow speed and pushing it along slowly. By this time, Andrews had run out of fuel and water. He could go no farther on the *General*, so he and his men took to the woods. They were captured, and Andrews and six others were hanged two months later. By that time the *General* was back in service, hauling hospital and ammunition trains. But it had been a near-run thing. Only the rain, which had hampered Andrews's efforts to destroy the bridges, and the tenacity of Conductor Fuller throughout the 100-mile chase, had saved the Confederacy from what one of its newspapers termed an attempt from which the '. . . mind and heart shrink back appalled at the bare contemplation. . . .'

Despite the failure of the Andrews raid, the Federals continued to regard the destruction of Confederate railroads as a major objective. Great opportunities were presented after they captured Vicksburg on 4 July 1863, because this success opened up to attack many key Confederate lines in Mississippi. The biggest of their attacks was on the Mississippi Central Railroad, and in particular on the locomotive depots at Canton, Winona and Grenada. However, because so many bridges had been destroyed already, the Federals were unable to remove the locomotives they captured at these places, and had to be content with kidnapping a number of locomotive men. Henceforth the Railroad was operated by the Confederates only in sections. In the south there were only two locomotives left, so a long stretch of line was reduced to fifteen round trips per month. Another section between two destroyed bridges had no locomotives at all, and was operated with horsedrawn cars. So depressing was the prospect for the railroads of this region that the Confederate General Pemberton ordered the demolition of all surviving rolling stock and locomotives. On this occasion the self-interestedness of the individual railroad managers was an asset, for one of them telegraphed a protest to the Confederate government, and the pessimistic general was overruled. The reprieved equipment was successfully evacuated to Georgia and the Carolinas later in the war, where it was put to good use.

On other fronts, the Confederate railroads were subject to raids by Northern cavalry wherever they were exposed. Even southern Virginia was not safe. Restoration of the damaged track was made more difficult by the Northerners' destruction of locomotive watering points, so that repair trains could only move with the assistance of local fire brigades. The Confederate repair gangs were always able to restore key lines, but it took time and the traffic lost was not made up. Moreover, the task absorbed resources of men and material from other projects which, though very promising, could not have top priority as a result. This was one reason why the Confederates made such little headway with the construction of new, strategically desirable, railroads.

The greatest railroad wrecker of all was General Sherman, whose famous march from Atlanta to the sea was virtually an orgy of railway destruction. Sherman had earlier gained experience with a deep raid eastwards from Vicksburg against the Confederates' few remaining railway facilities in eastern Mississippi. His target then was the settlement of Meridian, where three railroads joined and where there were, apart from railway installations, numerous warehouses full of military stores. However, his attack was carried out by infantry, too slow to achieve the necessary element of surprise. Indeed, the local Confederate officer in charge of transport had time to summon all available locomotives and cars to Meridian. In five days all the government stores had been evacuated, the last train departing within earshot of Sherman's advance troops. Sherman had to be content with seven days' careful destruction of the railroad installations of the locality; when he retired, about thirty miles of track had been completely destroyed, as well as more than fifty bridges. The Confederates restored the lines within six weeks, but during that time their army was irremediably weakened by the lack of supplies.

Sherman next turned his attention to the Confederates' Army of Tennessee. The line between the two sides cut the Western & Atlantic Railroad between Chattanooga and Atlanta, so that in

(overleaf) *The railroad terminal at Nashville, Tennessee, under Northern control in 1864. The rolling stock in the foreground bears the insignia of the United States Military Railroads*

the initial stages of the campaign both sides were supplied by trains of the same company. But whereas the southern segment of the railroad was decrepit, barely able to carry the most essential traffic, the portion of the line in Federal hands had been rebuilt by the Construction Corps and was backed up by a fine new workshop in Chattanooga. As Sherman advanced towards Atlanta his supply trains followed close behind, even though he was almost 400 miles from his base in Federal territory. One of his commanders happily reported after an action: '. . . while we were caring for the wounded, and bringing in Confederate prisoners, word was telegraphed from Resaca that bacon, hard-bread and coffee were already there at our service.' All this was in spite of the damage that the retreating Confederates had inflicted on the track. Even when the Confederates destroyed the 780-foot bridge over the Chattahoochie near Atlanta the Construction Corps had it in operation again within five days.

On reaching the outskirts of Atlanta, Sherman, as was his habit, avoided a costly battle and relied on attacks against the railroads supplying the city to force a Confederate withdrawal. His forces blocked the Georgia Railroad, the City's link with the east. Then his cavalry made a surprise raid on the Montgomery & West Point Railroad, used by the Confederates to bring food and ammunition from the south-west. The primitive strap rail of this line was easily torn up for about thirty miles, and the stations were burned. It took a month for the Confederates to restore operations, and during that time only a portion of the intended traffic got through, using a makeshift system of horse transport to bridge the gap. To the south, Sherman's cavalry raided the Macon & Western Railroad and the Central Railroad of Georgia, burning bridges and stations, wrecking track and water instal-lations and damaging any rolling stock they could find. At one station they captured a freight train and set its engine running, the steam regulator wide open, down the line towards the next station, where it ran into a Confederate passenger train full of refugees from Atlanta. Fortunately this train had an empty car at the rear, which, though totally destroyed, absorbed the shock and saved the passengers from serious injury.

Somehow, using worn-out materials, the Confederates patched up their southern lifeline and after a few days Sherman's officers could again hear the wail of Confederate locomotive whistles. It seemed that the Confederates would not be as easy to dislodge as the Northerners had hoped. Moreover, Sherman himself was dependent on one line of railroad, the Western & Atlantic, and, though this was well guarded and working efficiently with its new equipment, it was not immune to surprise cavalry raids, especially as it passed through hostile territory. Indeed, there was a serious Confederate cavalry attack on the railroad in August, in which thirty-five miles of reconstructed track were damaged and a new bridge at Etowah wrecked. But the Southerners were in too small a force to tarry long, and after their withdrawal the Construction Corps, backed by all the industrial resources the North enjoyed, soon had the trains running again.

Nevertheless, Sherman was worried by this attack, and speeded his moves against Atlanta, moving his right wing forward until it threatened to block the Macon & Western Railroad. At last the Confederates decided to withdraw. An attempt was made to carry away munitions and stores, but what was intended to be an orderly retreat soon degenerated into chaos. Over eighty boxcars, many of them loaded with government stores, were burned. Twenty-eight of them were loaded with ammunition, and they exploded spectacularly, only their wheels being left. Several precious locomotives were put out of action and left behind, among them the celebrated *General*.

But the Confederates continued their attacks on the Western & Atlantic Railroad, causing damage which, though temporary, was worrying to a general with an army of about 100,000 men already deep inside hostile territory. Sherman decided that he could not, after all, rely on this single-track line to sustain him for much longer. He decided to march through Georgia to the sea without the benefit of railborne supplies. During its last weeks, therefore, the W & A was kept busy bringing final consignments to Sherman and taking back all unnecessary material and men, as well as the wounded. Finally, Sherman gave the order to destroy the Railroad, so that the Confederates could not use it to pursue him, and so that it would remain out of action for months. Over eighty miles of track, some newly laid, were torn up and the rails heated and twisted. In the section closest to Northern territory it was possible to take the rails to safety, and the twice-rebuilt

(overleaf) *The Richmond & Petersburg Railroad, serving the Confederates' capital of Richmond, Virginia, was hard hit in 1865. This photograph was made in the Richmond depot at the end of the war*

bridge at Etowah was dismantled and its sections sent back. Finally the surviving railroad installations of Atlanta were burned or wrecked, and Sherman moved on.

Sherman did not deliberately follow the railroad routes on his march, but wherever he did approach them he ordered massive destruction. Rail was no longer heated and then manhandled round trees, but was twisted cold like a corkscrew by a specially designed machine. About 300 miles of track, vital to the Confederate war effort, was destroyed, only the occasional embankment and cutting remaining. Meanwhile, using railroads at a safe distance from Sherman, the Confederates tried to collect troops and concentrate them ahead of him, but their efforts were in vain, and Sherman entered Savannah at the end of the year. His destructive march had finally robbed the Confederates of their advantage of interior lines of communication. Later, when he turned northwards, he inflicted even more damage on the Southern railways.

Sherman's destructive march disheartened and disorganized the Southern war effort. In Virginia, General Lee, bereft of supplies and unable to create a miracle, surrendered at Appomattox on 9 April, 1865. In retrospect, it can be seen that the most successful generals of the Civil War, as in later wars, were those who first grasped the possibilities of the latest technology. In this war the latest technology was railway transport, and it is no coincidence that the generals whose reputations have not faded with the years—Sherman, Stonewall Jackson and Robert E. Lee— are precisely the generals whose strategies gave railroads a leading role.

Chapter 3

Railways in the Franco~ Prussian War

It was during the period of Bismarck's three wars that Prussia established its reputation as the leading proponent of the military uses of rail transport. To a large extent this reputation was exaggerated; as in other aspects of these wars, because Prussia was victorious, her mistakes went down in history as calculated risks, her confusions as spontaneity, and her refusal to learn lessons as steadiness of purpose.

Von Moltke, who became Chief-of-Staff at about the same time as Bismarck became Minister-President, had long been interested in the military use of railways. In 1843, already a rapidly rising young officer, he had written that: 'Every new railway development is a military benefit, and for national defence it is far more profitable to spend a few million on completing our railways than on new fortresses.' His appointment coincided with the introduction of a new conscription system. The Prussian army was proclaimed to be 'the Nation Armed'; henceforth conscription would in principle be extended to take in more of the eligible male age group, and after their service the conscripts would remain longer in the army reserve. The accumulation over the years of these trained reservists meant that the mobilized army would be much bigger. This scheme, which was later imitated by other European powers, made 'the people's war' a real possibility. It was a product of the railway age, for although it was workable without mechanical transport, the mass mobilization and concentration phases demanded the high-speed transport provided by railways to be really effective.

In her 1864 war against Denmark, Prussia made hesitating use of her railways to carry troops and supplies. Notably, an infantry division of 15,500 men and 4,600 horses was moved 175 miles from Minden to the outskirts of Hamburg in six days, using forty-two trains. Later, supplies were sent by rail from Hamburg into Schleswig-Holstein. The most important lesson from these tentative innovations was that congestion was most likely to develop at the unloading terminals. At the time it seemed that this lesson had been properly digested, because various experiments were carried out with mobile unloading ramps and with rear-end unloading. However, the very same difficulties occurred in Prussia's subsequent wars.

It was not this 1864 campaign but accounts of the American Civil War that inspired the creation in 1866 of the first Prussian railway troop units. Modelled on the US Construction Corps, and responsible for the destruction and repair of railways, they were at first purely skeleton organizations, only intended to be fully manned during hostilities. When war with Austria broke out in the summer of 1866, three of these railway troop sections were raised and put into the field. Each section had its own repair train, with a locomotive at each end. As this train pushed south along abandoned lines it was preceded by a hand trolley, propelled by four men and carrying an officer and bugler. On sighting a suspected obstruction the bugler would sound the alarm and the train would slow down to make a cautious approach. Normally cavalry outriders accompanied the train to scout for the possibility of ambush. Once the enemy had been sighted, the train would usually withdraw, pulled by the rear engine. At other times this locomotive was used for carrying messages to the rear. These railway sections were led by army engineer officers, but were mainly composed of various grades of Prussian State Railway employees, carefully selected for military service. The Austrians had nothing similar. Some Austrian officers had interested themselves in railway questions, but had received little encouragement from above, the War Minister considering that railway repair, even in wartime, was the business of the railway managements.

Although Bismarck's wars were premeditated, the Prussians mobilized later than their enemies on this occasion. To regain the lost time, von Moltke decided to use the railways to move his troops towards the Bohemian battleground. Since the lines radiated fanwise, so did the movement of the troops, so that on disembarking they formed an arc covering an unprecedentedly wide front of some 200 miles. As the Prussians won the war, this peculiar arrangement became known as von Moltke's 'strategy of external lines' and was repeated, for very similar reasons, in both 1870 and 1914.

In the first three weeks of the Prussian campaign, nearly 200,000 troops and 55,000 horses were efficiently deployed by the railways. But after this initial fine performance the railways were misused, when used at all. Von Moltke had not included supply trains in his mobilization timetable and his chief railway expert, instead of being retained in Berlin to sort out the inevitable muddle, was taken by von Moltke to the front. Thus there was no central direction; private contractors, in pursuit of profits and a reputation for patriotism, together with corps quartermasters looking to their career prospects, loaded and despatched supplies to the troops at a speed far greater than the goods could be delivered and unloaded at the other end. The resulting congestion meant that thousands of tons of supplies were held up *en route*. With the lines blocked by these trains of loaded freight cars, field officers could hardly be blamed for using railway cars as mobile storehouses; even if these cars had been unloaded they could not have been sent back for fresh loads. As the troops' food supplies rotted away in freight cars, field commanders ordered their units to live off the land, and felt free to cut themselves off from their railheads. It was this unexpected freedom of movement that helped them win the crucial battle of Königgrätz.

The Prussian commanders found that pursuit of the retiring Austrians by railway was impracticable. The line from Dresden to Prague would have been ideal for this purpose, but it passed within range of several Austrian fortresses that could only be overcome by protracted sieges. Rather than wait, the Prussians marched south with little help from the railway, and von Moltke wrote to Bismarck that it would be a good idea if future Prussian railways were laid to pass close to existing fortresses. Elsewhere, the Austrians haphazardly damaged the railways as they retreated. This destruction was not always effective. Sometimes bridges with charges already in place were not blown, and sometimes only one easily replaced span was destroyed. Lack of engineering experience, underestimation of the ease of restoring partially damaged structures, and emotional reluctance to destroy what were regarded as the technical achievements of the age seem to be plausible explanations of these failures. Presumably similar inhibitions were not felt by those Austrian officers who exploded mines for 250 feet along the tops of both sides of a key cutting. The dislodged rocks filled the cutting to a depth of six feet, but nevertheless a seventy-strong detachment of Prussians blasted their way through this obstacle in less than a day.

For von Moltke, the implied lesson of this campaign must surely have been that, mobilization apart, his new people's army could campaign very effectively without railway support. In retrospect, his final campaign under Bismarck, the Franco–Prussian, seems to have been based on this premise, even though subsequent accounts make different claims. Prussia's victory over the French has been largely attributed to the superiority of the Prussian railways, though, in fact, observers had previously regarded the French railways as strategically superior to the Prussian. In 1868 an anonymous German officer published *Die Kriegführung unter Benützung der Eisenbahnen*, in which he wrote that French troop trains were much faster because the French soldiers took their provisions into the train and did not, like the Germans, need to halt for meals. He also said that because France had only a few big railway companies, the French were more advanced in railway unification and standardization. Moreover, he added, four-fifths of the French network was double track, compared to a quarter in Germany, while French stations, being on average larger, could unload trains faster, and the French had more rolling stock per kilometre of line. Admittedly, at the same time there were French officers who, to stir up military and political opinion, asserted that the French railways were clearly inferior to Germany's, but foreign observers tended to agree that the balance of rail power was in favour of the French.

Von Weber, the Railway Minister of Saxony, was also concerned about the lack of uniformity among German railways. In 1870 he published a book about this very subject:

'... the military functionary is much more unfavourably placed. Every regulation which becomes known to him about the organization of the system, the station arrangements, the officials' uniforms, the signals, is only useful for the distance that he passes through with his troops for an hour or so; then there comes another railway, with its own, often very different, regulations.... At the big joint junction stations, where at

night the engineman sees a hundred different signals in be-
wildering confusion, resembling stars which, because of the
movement of the engine over the station curves, seem to move
backwards and forwards, merging into each other, you can
often find lines running close to each other on one of which a
white light means "stop" and on the other means "line clear"
... it would be to the general good in peacetime, and of
benefit to the military man in wartime, if the superintendent
met at Cologne was dressed like the superintendent at Königsberg, and if there was no danger of a Hamburg station inspector
being taken for a superintendent of the line by somebody from
Frankfurt.'

Undeterred by this lack of uniformity, the Prussian General
Staff had relied on the railways when drawing up their plans for
the war against France. Expecting that the French, who depended less on reservists, would take advantage of the longer
Prussian mobilization period by attacking first, von Moltke had
planned that his army would concentrate some way behind the
frontier. In order that this concentration should be effected with
speed and efficiency, highly detailed plans had been made over
the previous years. Six railway lines were available for the
Prussian forces, with three others for Prussia's allies from southern
Germany. This meant that no line needed to be used by more
than two corps. Each line was supervised by a Line Commission,
composed of military and railway officials. These Line Commissions were responsible for the co-ordination of military needs
with railway operating requirements. Their first major duty on
the outbreak of hostilities was to distribute the emergency
schedules to the key offices of their line. These schedules (*Fahrt-
Dispositionen*) were rather more than timetables; they not only
gave the schedule of the trains but also details of their com-
position, the number of men they would convey, the places where
coffee and meals would be served and the time allowed for these
halts. The execution of these schedules was to be so precise that
many trains would be able to make connections *en route*, dropping
and attaching cars to ensure that units would be complete, in their
order of battle, when their trains arrived at the concentration
areas.

Mobilization, during which Prussian reservists and soldiers on
leave returned to their regiments, lasted a week, ending on

26 July. On 22 July an Austrian newspaper correspondent passed through Cologne:

> 'The station was provided with a small guard, who in no way interfered with the movements of the many passengers. The station and restaurant were crowded with officers and soldiers of all arms, on their way to their regiments, and trains were loaded with unarmed men, who came from their various villages.'

On 24 July the railway companies began to reduce or cancel their ordinary train services in preparation for the concentration movement. This lasted eleven days, during which the troop trains carried over half a million men, together with horses and guns, to the concentration areas. The correspondent of *The Times* travelled from Berlin in one of the troop trains:

> 'We were told off to start with the gendarmerie of the Third Army Corps, which was already parading at the station. . . . Amid much enthusiasm our worthy gendarmes got into their carriages and we rolled out of Berlin. It rained in torrents. We reached Potsdam at 4.10. . . . At each halting-place the gendarmes get out and are made much of, patted on the back and forced to eat and drink—it must be forcing now—and strut their little minutes on the stage till the old colonel in command shouts out "*Einsteigen*", and in they get to the carriages, and move off amid cheers, and perhaps prayers, to the next station.'

It was this concentration that was the high point of the Prussian railways' wartime service (the Bavarian railways, whose military organization followed Prussian practice, did equally well). But after these initial three weeks, railway transport for the army was handled little better than in France. Part of the reason for the subsequent difficulties was that the troops had been despatched to the concentration areas with no provision for supply trains to follow them. They were expected to live on local supplies until train services could be arranged; it had been anticipated that the troop trains would demand so much track capacity that the scheduling of supply services would have been impossible until the troop movement ceased. Unexpectedly, the concentrated troops did not stand on the defensive, but rapidly moved forward into France to take advantage of their enemy's military ineptitude. In this way they soon widened the distance between their railheads and themselves, so that when supply trains did arrive at the appointed stations the distance remaining to be covered by horsedrawn transport was too great for effective distribution.

The strategy imposed by railway transport enabled the Prussian forces to dispense with the railway, once the concentration was achieved. This was because the distribution of the lines from the interior to the frontiers meant that concentration had to take place over a wide arc, so that the army could use the maximum number of lines. A very wide front was thus created, and with a wide front it was easier for troops to live off the land, which is what they did for most of the war. Great efforts were made to advance the railheads as the advance into France continued, but even at the end of the war, when Prussian troops had penetrated as far as the English Channel and western France, the number of lines which they could use effectively was small. In the early months several French fortresses blocked key main lines, so that through trains could not be operated by the Prussians. It was not until the fortress at Toul surrendered in September that the Prussian troops starting to lay siege to Paris could be supplied by through trains; even then the railway was mainly used to bring up guns and ammunition, the troops spending the early weeks of the siege gathering the local potato harvest. The line from the frontier to Paris via Rheims could not be used until the fortresses at Metz, Mezières and Rheims had been disposed of, and the line from the frontier at Mulhouse to Chaumont and Paris was blocked until the end of the war by the heroic defence of the fortress at Belfort.

One smaller fortified point, Bitche, did not surrender until after the end of the war. Its guns had prevented the Prussians using the peripheral Sarreguemines–Niederbronn line, and under the protection of these same guns fifteen French locomotives and a large quantity of rolling stock lay safe from Prussian hands throughout the war. The railways of Alsace were of little use to the invaders as long as the fortresses of Strasbourg and Schlestadt held out, so the German advance was on foot. By the end of October both these strongpoints were captured, and the first

(overleaf) At Munich in August 1870; an artist's impression of the departure to the front of Bavarian reservists. Although the vehicles are not accurately depicted, they are clearly an early version of the '40 men or 8 horses' regime

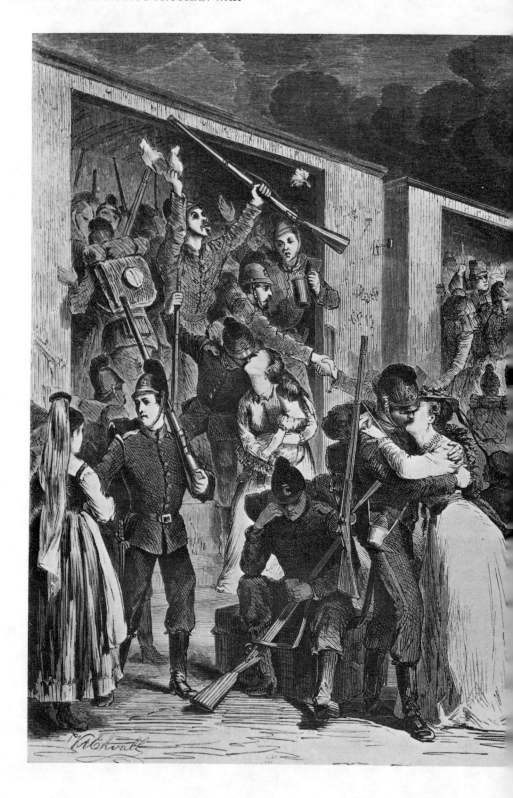

German trains could enter Mulhouse in mid-November. Mulhouse had finally been taken in early October; the Prussians had made several earlier entries, each of which had been registered by the local railway authorities, who would run the train service when the French held the city, and suspend it when the Prussians were in occupation.

The restrictive effect of enemy fortresses within range of main lines had already been noted in the war against Austria, and it is surprising that the Prussians were not better prepared for this. On the other hand, as events showed, the use of railways was not essential for their victory. But if the French had fought as well as had been expected, then the unavailability of rail transport could have put the Prussians into serious difficulty. On one or two occasions they did make efforts to re-route rail communication past fortresses. At Thionville they spent time and trouble linking industrial sidings to form an alternative route. But no sooner did the first train moving along this improvised line appear from behind a factory building than it was assailed by French artillery; only two trains were passed through safely, under cover of darkness. At Metz the Prussians were more successful, largely because on this occasion they had foreseen the problem and made preparations. They decided to build a 36-kilometre deviation line. Employing materials taken from captured French stocks, and three or four thousand troops and local peasants, they laid this line in six weeks. It was heavily graded because it crossed three valleys, and there were sharp curves. When the trains started to run they were limited to three or four vehicles. Even then derailments were frequent and the local soldiery began to call this line the 'Iron Cross Railway'. When the autumn rains came, operations were even more precarious, and after three weeks of work the only major construction of the line, a bridge over the Moselle, was washed away. On the same day, however, Metz capitulated, so the line was no longer needed.

French demolition also necessitated the construction of alternative routes. One of these was intended to circumvent the most notable of the French demolitions, that of the Nanteuil Tunnel. This tunnel, on the Rheims to Paris line, had its western end seriously damaged by French military engineers. They had excavated six mines, two at four metres from the entrance, two at twelve metres and two at twenty metres. These they had filled with powder (the French, unlike the Prussians, did not favour the

new-fangled dynamite). The resulting detonation brought down
the masonry for 25 metres and thereby admitted a downfall of
fine sand. The Prussians bored a narrow tunnel through this
packed sand, and might have succeeded in laying a single track
through it, but a heavy rainfall caused a fresh influx of sand and
clay, undoing two months' clearance work. It was then decided
to lay a deviation line of 5,000 metres. Labourers were brought
from Germany, the local inhabitants having refused to undertake
the work, and after three weeks the line was ready. Heavily
graded and very curved, it suffered a number of derailments, but
after a few weeks settled down into a more or less operable
condition. All the same the Prussian engineers gained little credit;
for over two months the line had been out of use while fruitless
clearance work proceeded. After the deviation had been finished,
the trains could run through to a railhead at Lagny, near Paris;
attempts to go beyond Lagny were thwarted by French artillery.
Another tunnel demolished by the French was at Montmédy.
This took the Prussians a month to clear, during which they discovered that the French had hidden eleven locomotives in the
tunnel. But the war ended before much use could be made either
of the tunnel or the locomotives.

In general, because rail transport was never crucial for the
operations of von Moltke's army inside France, the few lines laid
by his railway troops were themselves never of crucial importance
either. But after the war they were remembered by the French,
and it was seriously suggested that new railways of local
significance should be strictly limited because they might be used
by a future invader to circumvent French fortresses.

Both sides demolished a number of railway structures, not
always out of real necessity and not always very effectively. In the
first week of the war, when the Prussians were still expecting a
French attack, they partly demolished a bridge over the Rhine
near Strasbourg. This bridge, jointly built by the Est Railway
and the state of Baden, had been opened with great ceremony a
year previously, amid eloquent speeches about the role of railways as amicable links between nations. On the Est Railway
forty-six bridges and tunnels were totally or partially destroyed
during the war, and almost as many on the Nord Railway. When
the war spread to the west the Ouest and the Paris–Orleans
railways lost several key viaducts and bridges. On the Paris–
Lyons–Méditerranée Railway, fifteen major structures were

destroyed, eleven by the French and four by the Germans. Often destruction was only partial; the French in particular tended to blow up only the landward span or pile of a bridge, which the Prussians could repair within a few days. Sometimes commanders hesitated too long before issuing orders for the bridges to be blown, and sometimes orders issued in good time were not carried out. In one case, while engineers were inspecting a bridge prior to laying charges, the train which had brought them steamed off, taking their explosives with it. The removal of rail track was a fairly ineffectual measure. In theory it could prevent the advancing enemy using the railway to catch up with the retreating French, but in practice the Prussians never attempted to do this. In any case, restoring such track only demanded a few hours' effort, provided rails were available. This was usually the case, and when it was not, the Prussians did not hesitate to lift branch lines and sidings for the purpose. For example, after a major French defeat on 6 August, the railway centre at Hagenau was abandoned. The last French train left at 3 am, tearing up the tracks behind it, but at 10 am the next day the first Prussian train steamed in. Thirty German railway officials opened the line for business immediately, the first train being used to take back the wounded.

When the war started, the number of Prussian railway troop sections had been increased to four, and their Bavarian allies had another one. Each was of about 200 men and was well equipped for both destruction and repair. However, although they did good work they were inadequate for the tasks facing them. Unskilled labour had to be hired or brought in from Germany. The lack of uninterrupted rail routes inside occupied France, the need to guard the lines against attacks by French irregulars, rather frequent accidents, the flood of supplies sent from the German interior, the impossibly long distances between the railheads and the troops, and the different technical standards of the men and equipment brought in from the various German railways—all this combined to make the Prussian rail supply system ineffective. As in previous wars, train after train was despatched, only to be delayed for days or weeks by the increasing congestion on the approaches to the unloading points. Complete saturation, with stationary trains occupying all available sidings, reached far back into the home railway system, at least as far as Cologne and Frankfurt. In the first months of the war, until Metz was circumvented, the only line from Germany giving access to France was that from Landau to Nancy. This line became so congested that trains could take two days to cover the first thirty kilometres from Landau. Meanwhile only a trickle of trains actually reached the railheads. In the first few months of the war it is doubtful whether, on average, more than six supply trains reached the Prussian army in France each day. Later, in October, it was recorded that in four weeks an average of 7·2 trains were despatched daily from Germany to Nancy (and only 6·4 actually arrived). In an effort to free rolling stock, freight cars at one stage were unloaded *en route* irrespective of the destination of their cargoes. In many cases this meant that supplies had to be stored in the open, and there were several complaints about the stink of rotting meat. In an effort to meet this problem, von Moltke had already instructed his commanders in September to organize raids for the capture of French rolling stock.

Both in Prussia and the southern German states, train services

One of the most successful of French sabotage ventures: the locomotive Leisnig *poised on top of a sister-locomotive at Mézières in 1871, after the railway bridge had been blown up in front of a Prussian train*

4. Mézières. — Destruction du pont du Chemin de fer en 1871, avant le passage d'un train allemand

were reduced towards the end of 1870 to free resources for German railway operations in France. Because so many French railwaymen refused to work under Prussian occupation, German railwaymen were sent to France in numbers larger than anticipated. But Otto Corvin, correspondent of a Viennese newspaper, did not find this very helpful:

> 'The service on this road was a little better regulated than before, but everybody complained of the railroad *employés*, who seemed utterly demoralised by the war. As you might see in a train waggons belonging to many different railroad companies, you saw also *employés* in the most varied liveries. They had become very insolent and arbitrary; and though the passengers had to pay for their tickets, they were treated as if they were only parcels. . . . Whosoever did not use palm-oil did not get on. Whole waggons, loaded with goods, belonging to innocent people, who trusted to recommendations from head-quarters, and did not think of greasing the palms of the *employés*, disappeared as if by witchcraft, and I met many who had been running for weeks from station to station in search of them, whilst others who had expended a . . . note in the right place could have as many waggons despatched as they wanted. . . . I only pitied the poor innocent oxen and sheep, who had to remain standing in their waggon sometimes for forty-eight hours, without being fed or watered. It was indeed a pity to see the poor brutes, of which a large number died, and had to be thrown from the trains.'

Even though troop and ambulance trains were given precedence over supply trains, their operation was often inefficient. One Prussian instruction tried to improve this:

> '. . . All arriving trains must be unloaded as soon as possible, so that the empty trains can be sent back and newly-arriving trains enter the stations . . . infringements of this fundamental rule have been the cause of irregularities and interruptions, as well as the congestion encountered on the railways. . . . Most annoying delays and even the cancellation of entire trains have often been the result of troops not being in their places in good time. . . . All other considerations must be subordinated to the running of the trains. There will be no question of claiming, for example, that a departure can be delayed because troops have not finished their meal. If the time allowed is too short,

food can be distributed which the men can eat en route. . . .
If any person or object is left behind, the blame will always
attach to the commander. . . .'

Although the invading armies were able to make do without
significant assistance from the railways—thanks to their ability to
live off the land, their unexpectedly small expenditure of ammunition, and the poor showing of the French army—at the time
many Prussian officers were very nervous, having been well
indoctrinated with the importance of railways in wartime. So
when a bridge at Fontenoy-sur-Moselle, on the key line between
Nancy and Toul, was attacked and destroyed by the French, the
Prussians soon took counter-measures. What made this destruction
particularly irritating was that this main line, promising direct
rail access from Germany to Paris, had only just been opened to
German traffic by the capture of the French fortress at Toul.
Guerillas, the so-called *francs-tireurs*, were blamed for this act, and
this provided a pretext for the use of measures which were
regarded as atrocious not only by foreign observers but also by
many Prussian officers. With no convincing evidence in support,
the local Prussian administration announced that the village of
Fontenoy had sheltered the alleged guerillas. This village was
burned. At the same time the increasing number of accidents was
blamed on the activities of *francs-tireurs*. Although it was true that
francs-tireurs had taken the occasional pot-shot at Prussian trains,
and had removed the occasional rail, and would later progress to
detonating charges beneath trains, the majority of mishaps were
due to natural causes; the Prussian railway operators were working in a strange country with strange equipment, receiving little
help from French railwaymen, and often suffering from exhaus-
tion. In such conditions accidents were inevitable. The *francs-
tireurs* could, for example, hardly be blamed for the number of
chimneys knocked off Prussian locomotives drafted to France;
Prussian planners had failed to notice that bridges were lower on
French railways than they were in Germany.

One of the more spectacular successes of the *francs-tireurs* was
the blowing up of a troop train between Rheims and Metz in
October 1870. They inserted thirty kilogrammes of powder
beneath the track, and an ordinary shell, held upright with its
nose touching the bottom of a rail, was used as detonator. The
weight of the locomotive depressed the rail and thereby ignited

The two-piece chimney as fitted to Royal Prussian State Railways locomotives, after mishaps during the Franco-Prussian War had demonstrated the inconvenience of using locomotives too tall for the French railways' clearances

the charge. The train was thrown down an embankment and the seventy-five Frenchmen waiting in ambush opened fire. This virtual massacre of helpless troops was regarded by the Prussians as an atrocity, and no doubt encouraged them to take further retaliatory measures.

A policy of reprisals, such as the Prussians adopted, was understandable to the extent that the operations of the *francs-tireurs*—men who fought without wearing an appropriate uniform—also seemed, in the military tradition of the time, to be themselves atrocious. But the open attribution of all kinds of hackle-raising activities, like the derailment of hospital trains, to the *francs-tireurs*, was less excusable. In general, both the Prussians and the French found it convenient to exaggerate the importance of the movement. For the Prussians, it was a good way of mollifying critics of their policies. The figure of 100,000 Prussian *Landwehr* troops needed to guard the railways in France was widely quoted at the time and has not been effectively challenged since, although it, too, seems to be an exaggeration.

The Prussian administration in Lorraine promised immediate death for 'any persons not belonging to the French army and not showing external indications of being a soldier . . . who destroy bridges, canals, telegraphs or railways. . . .' What captured the imagination of the world, though, was a measure at first published at Nancy, and later elsewhere in eastern France:

'Several cases of damage having been inflicted on the railways, the commander of the 3rd German Army has issued the order that trains are to be accompanied by local inhabitants, well-known and well-considered locally. These inhabitants will be placed on the locomotive, so as to make it clear that any accident caused by the hostility of the inhabitants will, in the first place, strike one of their own nationals. Prefects are requested to organise, in conjunction with railway management and railway transport officers, a regular accompaniment service.'

Within a day or two the most respected inhabitants of Nancy were receiving notices reading:

'Monsieur . . . is invited to present himself, on receiving this, to the railway station of Nancy, at the disposition of the undersigned, in order to accompany, as a security measure, the train leaving at . . . hours . . . minutes for . . . . . . In case of refusal, the gendarmerie will use physical means.'

Not all the local authorities carried out this measure to the full. One prefect put a hostage on just one train. Another announced that he hoped it would not be necessary to put the order into effect. On several trains the hostage was invited into the carriage reserved for Prussian officers; evidently many of them felt ashamed of the order and tried to make things easier for the hostages. It was, after all, the harsh winter of 1870–71 that witnessed this display of local notables on passing locomotives. That not a single hostage came to any harm was taken by some to prove that the measure was completely effective and therefore justified. More likely, it merely showed that *francs-tireur* attacks on trains were much less frequent than had been claimed.

Contrary to popular impressions at the time, the French railways responded superbly to the demands of the 1870 war. At a time when military affairs were blatantly mismanaged by what seemed to be a collective leadership of Parisian newspaper editors, vociferous politicians, bickering generals, the Emperor Napoleon III and his Empress Eugénie, the railway companies were almost alone in carrying out what they promised. Yet because of governmental and military mismanagement, the rail transport of men and supplies was all too frequently confused.

So the French railways could not win the war. But, in one sense, they did win the peace. The thirst for scapegoats, after the war had come to a humiliating end, might have been expected to cast the railways as the cause of the French disasters. After all, the railway companies had long been unpopular among the French, largely for internal political reasons. In 1870–71 Frenchmen had heard all kinds of tales, mainly true, about the chaos prevailing on the railways serving the troops. When unsuccessful generals launched a deluge of post-war memoirs they rarely failed to contrast the allegedly poor performance of the French railways with the allegedly faultless performance of the Prussian railways. But what was remarkable about this war was that memoirs were written not only by the generals but also by several railway managers. In time, because the railwaymen could marshal so many examples of military incompetence, it was their view of events which prevailed, and the Ministry of War set about preparing proper regulations for the use of rail transport in a future war. By 1914, the French were able to use their railways as effectively as any other of the great powers.

One War Minister, General Niel, had in fact attempted in 1869 to bring the regulations for the use of railways up to date. These regulations had remained practically unchanged since the days of the 1859 Italian campaign, in which the army had been so successful in moving troops that it ignored the serious deficiencies in its transport of supplies. The premature death of Niel and the 1870 war forestalled a definite adoption of the proposals suggested by the commission he had set up. However, the commission was not completely ignored, for several of its suggestions were provisionally adopted on the eve of the war. Not all of them were directed at what outside observers would have considered to be major problems; one recommendation was as follows:

Method for Making Coffee

A receptacle of at least 150 litres is to be taken, in which sugar, coffee and water are placed, with each ration of 24 grams of coffee and 31·05 grams of sugar being allowed 42 centilitres of water. By means of a copper tube of diameter 0·012 metres fitted to a locomotive pressure gauge, a jet of steam is directed into the receptacle, with the tube deep in the water so as to agitate all the liquid. The operation is finished when the steam no longer dissolves. . . . The coffee is made before the arrival

of the troops. Distribution must commence without delay. . . .
The receptacles are provided by the military administration,
the copper tubes by the railway companies.

When the first emergency orders on the Est Railway went out
during the night of 15 July, 1870, the fifth in order of priority
concerned the provision of copper tubes for making coffee.

In France's three great modern European wars—those of 1870,
1914–18 and 1939–40—it was the Est Railway that carried the
main burden of supplying the troops. This railway, a private
company in the first two of the wars and a region of French
Railways in the third, serves the area between Paris and the
Rhine. In the nineteenth century, and to some extent even now,
this region was the French army's base in both war and peace,
with its garrison towns, fortifications and training grounds. The
Paris terminus, the Gare de l'Est, became the traditional point of
farewell for soldiers destined for the front, and has been the
setting for many patriotic paintings. However, on 16 July, 1870,
when the first emergency troop train left for the front, the glow on
the soldiers' cheeks was more alcoholic than patriotic.

The Est Railway, together with its neighbours—the Nord and
Paris–Lyon–Méditerranée railways—was informed of the emergency on 15 July, and during the following night issued the
necessary instructions to its staff. They were to cancel the
departure of all freight trains, to unload all covered and flat
freight cars, to double the strength of telegraph operators, to
reduce the passenger services on all lines to one or perhaps two
trains a day, with these retained trains giving priority to mail
services, to provide coffee services and horse-watering facilities
for troop trains *en route*, and to distribute timetables for military
trains. The first troop train was scheduled to depart at 5.45 pm
from the Gare de l'Est on 16 July. However, the troops destined
for this train arrived at the terminus at 2 pm, because the military
had decided that they would be issued with blankets in the station
courtyard. Distribution completed, the men were allowed to
wander off until train time. Most went to neighbouring bars and
taverns, and were so intoxicated when they returned to the
station that the train could only be loaded and despatched with
great difficulty. Some, moreover, had been relieved of their
ammunition by citizens who felt that the war might provide good
opportunities to bring fire to bear on their own government.

The next day, 17 July, the Est Railway operated forty-nine troop specials to the concentration areas of Metz and Strasbourg. Departures were split between Paris and Châlons, the latter being an intermediate station serving encampments of the standing army. In Paris itself, to avoid congestion of the Gare de l'Est, many trains were despatched from the suburban stations of Pantin and La Villette. Pantin was reserved for artillery and engineer units, whose embarkation proceeded almost without a hitch, possibly because it was in those two branches of the service that the most intelligent officers were to be found. At the Gare de l'Est, however, units arrived hours too early or too late for their allotted trains, and were accompanied on to the platforms by inebriated mobs singing patriotic songs. Trains allotted to particular units were either despatched half-empty or had their spare capacity filled by other units, creating great problems at the arrival stations. Although no timetables had been prepared before the war, the Niel commission had ensured that some general principles had been agreed, so the Est Railway managers had little difficulty in planning schedules. But provision of the necessary locomotives, rolling stock and train crews was more difficult, achieved only after heroic hard work and overtime.

Since the French army was smaller but quicker into the field than the Prussian, the French strategy was to invade Germany before the Prussians could properly mobilize and deploy their reservists. This was a risky strategy, but it might have won the war if only the French railways had been properly used. But they were not; the trains were provided, but the military made poor use of them. A basic error was the combination in one movement of the two procedures of mobilization and concentration. This meant that formations could be incomplete when they marched up to the departure station. In theory they were followed by their later units, but in practice the laggard units or individuals often failed to make contact with their parent formation. As General Chareton later pointed out to the National Assembly:

'You could see your railway trains encumbered by men criss-crossing their way in all directions and in all parts of France, often arriving at their destination just when the corps to which they belonged had left, then running after this corps, only to catch it up when it was beaten, in retreat, or besieged in an inaccessible fortress.'

The 2nd Bavarian Army Corps, en route to France, makes a refreshment stop at Darmstadt in August 1870

At all the stations in and behind the war zone individual soldiers became part of the so-called *masse flottante*, having abandoned the search for their units. They crowded into station buffets where they were served endless free drinks by women's voluntary organizations. In time they became a threat to discipline; at Rheims, several hundred of them banded together to pillage stationary freight cars. The Ouest and Paris–Orleans railways meanwhile transferred locomotives and rolling stock to the eastern railways. During the first three weeks of the war about 300,000 men were conveyed, as well as 65,000 horses, 6,600 guns and carriages, and 4,400 supply and munition carts. In these operations there were only two train accidents, both collisions, in which two soldiers were seriously injured and others slightly hurt. In addition there were forty-two personal accidents, mostly to soldiers who, having insisted on travelling on the train roof, failed to notice low bridges. Casualties would have been higher had it not been for the slowness of the trains; to enhance line capacity, allow for delays, and ensure that trains would not be beyond the power of their locomotives, the Niel commission had standardized schedules, stipulating rather slow speeds for each section of the line.

Within ten days of mobilization, the French were able to have 86,000 men at the frontier, at a time when hardly any Prussian soldiers had been moved to the German side of the border. But in the following ten days, while the Prussians were bringing up their complete formations to the front, the French units were still half-complete, marching and counter-marching in search of their camps, their supplies, their straying units and often their officers.

The first and the greatest case of chaos at the receiving stations occurred right at the start of the campaign. The congestion at Metz was regarded for decades afterwards as a textbook example of how not to operate a wartime railway. When the first trains of infantry arrived in Metz no order had been issued as to their ultimate destination, so the troops had to wait several hours in the station. The men were allowed to leave the trains, but the baggage cars were not unloaded. As trains followed one another into the station they had to be put on to sidings, much to the annoyance of the officers in charge of the baggage. Sometimes whole regiments were held up in the station for five or six hours. However, the confusion attending the arrival of the troop trains was nothing compared to the situation which developed when the supply trains began to steam into the yards. The local railway administration discovered that it had to deal with two sets of army supply officers, each with different ideas. The local supply officers, based on Metz, had received no instructions concerning the incoming trains and could give railwaymen no indications of what to do with the supplies. The divisional supply officers, who arrived with the troops, claimed authority over these supplies, but since they had not been told the ultimate destination of their units, they were unwilling to unload the cars in case they were then ordered to move on farther. Railway officials, besides endeavouring to find destinations for this freight, at the same time had to respond to supply officers who arrived at the station in search of particular commodities that had been despatched to them but which had been side-tracked in some unrecorded spot. A high official of the Est Railway, Jacqmin, later wrote:

'One supply officer despatches freight without knowing, and without being able to know, if another supply officer is able to receive it. One staff officer comes to seek out some oats, while another claims camping equipment. Each one asserts that his instructions are of the greatest urgency and that the success of the campaign depends on their prompt execution. Add to this confusion already caused by the multiplicity of orders, the demands of the artillery which designates the tracks which it alone can use, and which wants to convert stations into arsenals, and the supply service which wants to convert them into storehouses. . . . The greatest confusion soon reigned in the station. . . . One other great difficulty was imposed on the Company. It was told to keep at Metz the necessary stock for the immediate transfer of an army corps of 30,000 men. To do this, about 40 trains had to be immobilized, distributed at nearby stations in Frouard and Thionville. One night, the order was given to carry out this move. In four hours everything was ready, the locomotives with steam up, the train crews at their posts. Nobody turned up. There was a counter-order. Twice the same *tour de force* was achieved, and twice it was to no purpose. Twice, consequently, railway supply operations were suspended needlessly.'

Eventually, not only was every available siding in the vicinity blocked with loaded cars, but also some of the through lines. Unloading was at length organized by the railway company itself, since the army authorities seemed paralysed. Freight cars were unloaded where they stood, their contents put on the ground beside them, and a start made in sending the empty cars back. But shortage of freight handlers delayed the process. The army would not provide any labour for this work; in Metz itself only the Imperial Guard was billeted, and the Imperial Guard was a privileged corps not likely to soil itself with non-military labour. Thus when Metz was at length surrounded there still remained hundreds of loaded freight cars which, in due course, were captured by the Prussians.

Despite their own worries, the railways rescued the army from the consequences of its mistakes on several occasions. Often their initiatives were undertaken without any military help or encouragement. During the German advance local railway administrations usually succeeded in removing locomotives and rolling stock despite the army's reluctance to inform them of impending retreats. Usually, too, local railway officials were a surer source of information than the military despatches, especially when the situation was grim. Railwaymen were sometimes the first to discover the latest extent of a German advance, and more than once local military commanders, without orders from their own higher command, were able to take defensive measures on the basis of information telegraphed down the railway lines.

In evacuations, the railways were expected to operate until the very last moment, and even when their services were no longer required the military authorities seemed reluctant to order the railwaymen to join the withdrawal. In the case of telegraphists, who were expected to stay at their posts until the Prussians arrived, and then to destroy their instruments, this seems justified. But the railway managers were surely right to order withdrawals in other cases. When the city of Nancy was evacuated by the army on 11 August, about 100 locomotives and thousands of freight cars were left behind, and in the two days between the departure of the French troops and the arrival of the Prussians, the local railwaymen sent all this valuable material to the rear. Just one old locomotive was left, and the Prussians found this useful only for heating their men's soup. During the war the Prussians captured only about eighty French locomotives, whose evacuation, almost always, had been forbidden by French officers.

It is in retreat that the utilization of rail transport becomes most difficult. Anticipated loading points are abandoned before the trains can reach them; lines essential to the timetable are cut by the enemy; the morale of both soldiers and railwaymen becomes frayed. The movement of three army corps by the French railways after the abandonment of Nancy was therefore a considerable achievement. Prussian writers later said that the Prussian railways would not have been able to carry out this operation, which, being essentially a turning movement, changed the strategic picture while preserving the demoralized French troops from the confident Prussians and blocking the approaches to Paris. The three corps were disembarked between Châlons and

Rheims ready to fight (not too successfully) another day. It was during this evacuation and redeployment operation that railway officials reported Prussian cavalry near a vital junction. On this occasion the army responded by sending a protective force, which held the line until after the last train had passed. It was while this complex movement was occupying all the attention of the Est Railway management that one of the War Ministry's departments ordered an immediate supply of freight cars to transport a special high-grade iron needed to make barrack roofs, an incident that received wide post-war publicity as an example of ministerial lack of imagination.

One of the most striking examples of ineptitude in the handling of French transport occurred at the very end of the war, when the eastern town of Dôle was threatened with capture by the Prussians. There were over 500 freight cars at Dôle that had to be evacuated to Besançon. However, Besançon was congested with cars which the military quartermasters refused to unload, and moreover was expecting evacuation trains from other directions. The desperate expedient of converting one of the two through lines at Besançon into a storage siding was therefore adopted. However, this effort to make space for the cars from Dôle by converting a double track line to single track virtually prevented the Dôle cars from reaching Besançon; they were halted between the two centres, effectively preventing further movement. The military authorities then decided to send these cars in the opposite direction, to Dijon. But one hour after issuing the appropriate order, they reconsidered the decision and sent a second order. This was to instruct the railway to sort the freight cars and to send to Dijon only those cars laden with food and fodder. The railwaymen at Dôle immediately began to do so, only to receive a third order cancelling this process and instructing that all the cars be sent to Besançon after all. With a good deal of difficulty, amid the congestion, locomotives were sent from one end of their trains to the other, and another attempt to reach Besançon was made. But then news came that the Prussians were only fourteen kilometres distant. This meant that Dijon had become the only possibility. The locomotives were once again shifted, and the first train moved off. The second train, ready after about an hour, was struck by a Prussian shell fired at a range of only half a mile. Nevertheless, it got away, and so did several other trains. Working under fire, the railwaymen managed to despatch almost 400 cars before the advanced units of the Prussian forces entered the station.

Political rather than military vacillation was to blame for the confusion on the Est Railway in August 1870, when the mutinous *Garde Mobile*, encamped at Châlons and causing all kinds of trouble, was scheduled for removal. These units had only recently arrived from Paris, where their departure had already been the occasion for minor rioting. The War Ministry advised the Est Railway that the eighteen battalions would not be returned to Paris, where they could have a damaging effect on morale, but would be divided between various towns and villages in the north. However, since they would probably refuse to get into the trains if they were aware of this, these were to point towards Paris, and would be re-routed northwards on reaching the outskirts of the capital. As each battalion consisted of 900 men, the Railway lost no time in arranging this movement. On 17 August the ministry confirmed the arrangements, adding that nobody should be allowed to leave the trains; presumably it realized that when the trains were being switched outside Paris, the *Garde* might well decide to leap out. How the Est Railway officials were to prevent this armed horde from doing what it pleased was not stated. In any case, on the same day the Railway received from its officials in the Châlons area assurances that the planned move would not take place, since the men had already discovered that a plot was being hatched against them. On the next day the Railway found itself the recipient of contradictory orders. The order from Paris to carry the men north still remained in force, but the local command had instructed the Railway to entrain the men at Rheims and carry them to Paris. Eventually the War Ministry cancelled its original instructions. Meanwhile, the local military commander in Paris was consulted by the Company. He professed to be completely ignorant of the whole affair, but was greatly alarmed at the prospect of the *Garde Mobile*, after disembarking at the Gare de l'Est, marching through the city towards the camp allotted to it. It was left to the Railway officials to make the obvious suggestion that the trains should take them direct to the camp, which was situated not far from one of their main lines. This is what happened, to the relief of many.

In that same month, August, the correspondent of the *Manchester Guardian* travelled to the front from Paris:

'. . . our delays grow more serious and longer, till we reach Commery, where we encounter a tedious one of two long hours' duration caused by the collision of two trains in front of us laden with troops. . . . Starting again, we creep slowly on until we reach Toul, the scene of the disaster. Here the line is torn up, and strewn with fragments of carriages, some shivered into splinters, and others bent and broken into the most erratic shapes. The shock must evidently have been a very violent one, and the damage to the occupants severe, but to what extent it was quite impossible to ascertain, the reticence of a French official being utterly unassailable. He takes off his hat, rubs the back of his bristly head, shrugs up his shoulders, and exclaims "Dieu-de-dieu-de-dieu". . .

'After a weary while we, whose baggage causes us to remain with the train, arrive at Frouard too, to find this, the junction with the main line for Metz, in what our conductor calls "a fog of trains".

'On they come in a seemingly never-ending line, each train consisting of sixty or seventy carriages, and each drawn by two of the enormous engines built by "His Excellency M. Schneider", at Creuzot. Even they, powerful as they are, are hardly able to start their heavy-laden load. On they come, now a tall dark train of covered luggage vans, filled with men, and looking like steam hearses, now a white-shrouded train of ambulance waggons and litters, suggestive of a very harrowing consequence of the pomp and circumstance of war; now a singing crowd of soldiers, who have decked their train with huge branches of willows, cut from the marshy lands where they were last encamped.'

The assumption that trains could be made to operate simply by issuing orders was never abandoned by some high officers, even after painful experience. Such experiences resulted not in a questioning of assumptions but in criticisms of railway administrations. In 1870, the Paris–Lyons–Méditerranée Railway was the victim of this attitude, when in the afternoon of 16 November it received an order to transport an army corps 262 kilometres from Chagny to Gien, the move to commence the following morning and to be finished the day after. Thus the company was required to move 40,000 men as well as several thousand horses within thirty-six hours. Moreover, Chagny was a station with very few loading platforms, and as a result of a previous evacuation, it possessed very little spare rolling stock. Out of the fifty special trains required, Chagny had enough stock to form just two, and it would take at least one day to bring in enough extra stock and locomotives from the nearest main centres, about 200 kilometres away.

The management did what it could. It had two possible single-track routes between the two points and decided to use the shortest of these for the loaded trains, and to return the empty stock for reloading via the longer route. In effect, it created a double-track route in place of two single-track routes, and thus increased the total line capacity available. The movement was finished in the evening of 19 November. Eighty-eight trains were loaded because more troops appeared than the high command had expected. Since the first of the four days was occupied with empty stock movements, this implied an average of up to thirty trains each day, an exceptional achievement; the Prussians reckoned that fourteen trains per day was about the maximum feasible.

The siege of Paris demonstrated that railway companies, even without trains to run or lines on which to run them, could still be a considerable military asset. In the first place they were organizations; they had the men, the administration and often the material to get things done. This was demonstrated in many ways, not the least being the transport service operated by the railways within Paris, using their 2,500 draught horses. Railway workshops, with their trained technicians and disciplined workers, were ideal for manufacturing and repairing weapons and for making ammunition. Armoured trains were also built; the latter took part in three of the battles on the city outskirts and could probably have done more if they had been used more boldly. Stations and offices were converted into hospitals, served by railway personnel, and some large stations were converted into flour mills, powered by driving belts attached to locomotives. The terminals of the Est and Orleans railways had another use; having large covered areas they were ideal for the manufacture of the observation and communications balloons used by the defenders. Several of the balloon launchings were made from the station forecourts.

It was in this war that the ambulance train, hitherto regarded as an experimental novelty, became an established and widely used means of coping with the problem of the battlefield wounded. Napoleon Bonaparte, in one of those utterances so treasured by his admirers, once said that he preferred a dead soldier to a wounded one, but he did not have the benefit of railway transport to rid himself of those who had been maimed in his service. The wounded not only cluttered up the front line, demanding attention, supplies, hospitals and doctors, but, in the insanitary field hospitals they tended to develop diseases that could later be communicated to the fit men. As the railway age progressed, so did medical science, and by mid-century it seemed likely that soldiers transported rapidly from the front to rear hospitals would be less likely to develop diseases and more likely to undergo operations which could not be attempted in front-line hospitals.

Strictly speaking, the first railway ambulance trains were the wagons of the Balaclava Railway during the Crimean War, which instead of returning empty sometimes brought out the walking wounded. No doubt this was a terrible journey for them, but it was better than horse and cart, the only alternative. In the French and Piedmontese campaign against the Austrians in 1859, a war in which the wounded were so badly treated that the first steps towards the Geneva Convention soon followed, both sides used ambulance trains. These consisted of freight cars whose floors were covered with straw or palliasses. The jolting of these cars could only have been agonizing, and much subsequent thought was given to the best way of loading and transporting the wounded.

The experience of the American Civil War had surprisingly little effect on European thinking about ambulance trains. The Americans had tried a variety of methods of solving the basic problem, that of stowing the wounded in as efficient and as comfortable a manner as possible. The Americans, too, had introduced the concept of the hospital train, in which the wounded could be tended *en route* by doctors and nurses, and could be fed proper food and drink from the train's own resources. In this the Americans had been aided by the nature of their rolling stock; the broad doors of boxcars and the central aisles of passenger cars both provided better opportunities for good stowage than the

(overleaf) *Experience painfully gained in the Franco-Prussian War was embodied in the design of later ambulance trains. This picture shows part of a 3-ward ambulance train built in the First World War by the Lancashire & Yorkshire Railway*

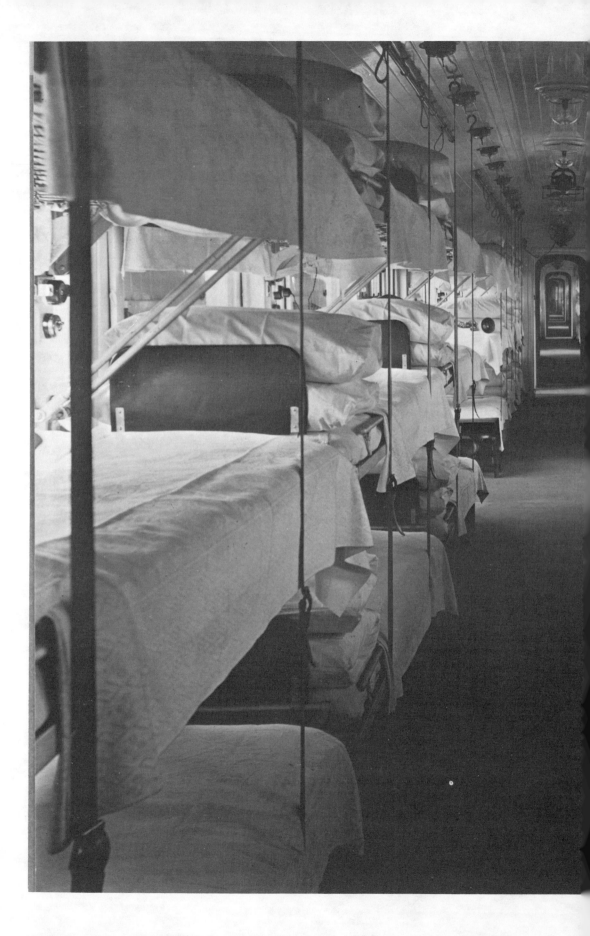

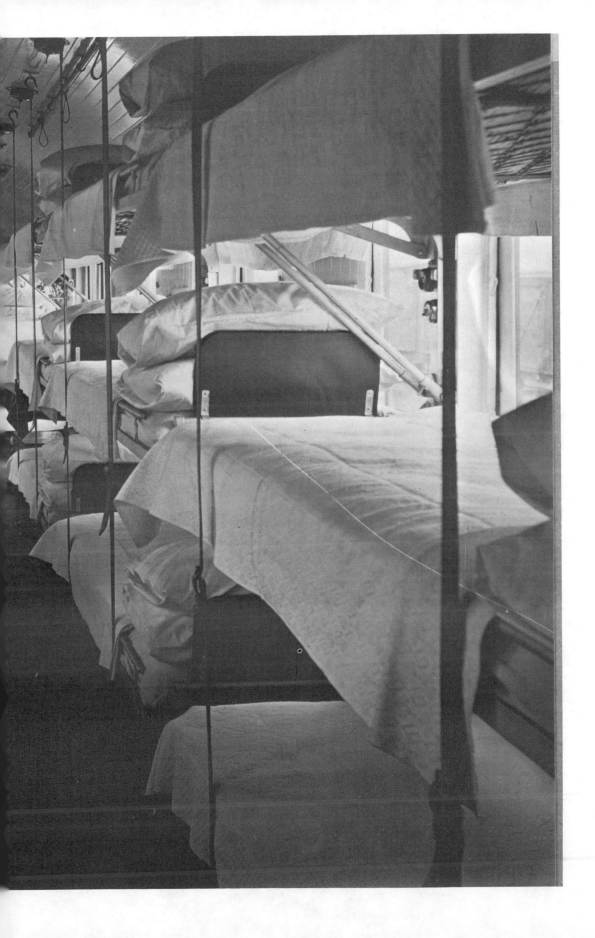

European type of vehicle. Finally, the Americans had shown what could be done when mass movement of wounded was necessary; after the Battle of Gettysburg, for example, over 15,000 wounded were despatched by Federal trains within three weeks, mostly to well-equipped hospitals in the big cities.

But in Prussia's wars against Denmark and Austria a few years later it seemed that the benefits of American experience had been ignored. Rules laid down in 1861 were still in force, and the Prussian wounded suffered accordingly. After the Battle of Königgrätz thousands of wounded lay on the battlefield for up to three days, and then those who were taken by train to Dresden or Berlin, often with their wounds still undressed, were delayed by railway congestion for several more days. Those days were passed in passenger cars (for the sitting wounded) or on the straw-covered floors of freight cars (for the more seriously wounded). Sometimes the vehicles were stationary for hours, and when they did move the jolting could be agonizing. Yet even bearing in mind the large number who died unnecessarily in these trains, and the discomfort of those who survived, the wounded were still far better off on the railways than they would have been in field hospitals.

The pressure brought to bear by Prussian public opinion, incensed by the sufferings of the wounded, was one reason for the Prussian General Staff's reappraisal of its ambulance train regulations after the war. A commission set up in 1867 heard evidence from a Kiel University surgeon, who strongly recommended the American system for the long-distance movement of wounded; that ambulance vehicles should have end doors and gangways, so that the medical staff could go down the train to attend the wounded even while the train was in motion; that the wounded should be brought to the trains on stretchers which could be fixed inside the rail vehicles, and thereby avoid the danger and pain of transferring the wounded from stretcher to bunk or mattress; and that the trains should have proper accommodation for medical and catering requirements. To some extent these recommendations were implemented. The Prussian Railways henceforth built its 4th class passenger cars with end doors, so that they could easily be converted for hospital train use; the 4th class vehicles were chosen because they had no seats, and it was therefore easy to refit them to carry stretchers.

The method of stowing the wounded continued to be the

subject of many experiments in various countries after the Franco–Prussian War. By 1914 both the French and the British used portable iron frames that could be installed in freight cars and on which two tiers of stretchers could be attached. The flexibility of the iron, and the use of sprung fittings, absorbed most of the shocks caused by the rail joints. For some time after the Civil War, the Americans favoured the use of rubber loops, into which the stretcher handles could be inserted. In Germany and elsewhere there was for some time a preference for a method in which the stretchers were suspended like hammocks. However, in practice this method often meant that stretchers would be knocked against the sides of the vehicle when high speed or rough track was encountered. The Russians developed a method in which the stretchers were suspended on springs. This certainly eliminated the jolts, but it was not unknown for the wounded to find themselves trampolining at certain speeds.

The Boer War and the Russo–Japanese War aroused great public interest in ambulance trains. Or rather, the press chose to describe these trains in great detail because there was often little else cheerful to write about. The care of the wounded was a comforting topic when the reality of war without victory provided little material for rousing articles. The ambulance trains, too, were a fitting occupation for the royal ladies. In both Britain and Russia the princesses and their mothers would provide and fit out these trains, sometimes even serving as nurses themselves.

Chapter 4

Railways as a Third Arm

The construction of new railways to supply advanced troops was a task in which the Prussians had not been too successful during their war against France. The few short lines which they laid were built slowly and were of low technical standard. It was the Russians, in their 1877–78 campaign against the Turks, who showed what could be achieved in this field.

Russia had made considerable preparations for this war, and on the eve of hostilities obtained the right to use Romanian railways for military trains. However, this was not as great an advantage as it seemed, for the Romanian railways were very few, rather badly built, and of standard gauge as opposed to the broader Russian gauge. It was not long, therefore, before the Russians decided to build their own lines. The first of these was outside Romania, connecting Russia's South Western Railway with the Romanian frontier at Galatz. This line had already been planned as a commercial enterprise, but to speed construction the projected route was changed, and a longer alignment through easier terrain was selected. The single-track line of 189 miles was laid in just over three months, an achievement carefully noted in the war ministries of other powers. Since the labour force had refused to work on holy days, of which there had been no fewer than forty-two during those three months, the achievement was even more remarkable than it appeared on paper. The work had been put out to the contractor Polyakov, who in modern textbooks is regarded as something of an infamous entrepreneur, but who enjoyed at that time a reputation for energy and expedition.

While the construction was proceeding Polyakov addressed himself to many of the locomotive builders of Europe, in a mostly successful endeavour to find suitable engines for the new line. When finished, the line could carry seven pairs of trains daily, and after the war it was absorbed into the Russian railway network. A second new line was built inside Romania, to provide a link with a bridge built by the Russians over the Danube at Simitza. This was completed less rapidly, its construction held up by the very difficulties which had made a railway essential. In particular, the existing roads were overloaded and disintegrating under military traffic, so it was only with long delays that the materials for the new railway could be brought up. The third line in Romania was, for similar reasons, not finished when the war ended.

The South Western Railway bore the brunt of the wartime traffic, and was fiercely criticized for its alleged inefficiency. It already had a bad reputation among the military, earned when a troop train plunged into a ravine after some track workers had forgotten to replace a rail that they had removed from the main line. Much of the wartime trouble encountered by this company was a consequence of the gauge difference at the frontier; the delays imposed by transhipment meant, among other things, delays in the return of vitally needed empty rolling stock. Eventually one line, from Ungeni to Jassy, was converted to mixed gauge by the addition of a third rail, but this conversion, being short, merely provided more line for transhipment operations. When eyewitnesses reported Russian wounded being 'stacked like logs' waiting for ambulance trains, public opinion, looking for a scapegoat to alleviate the distress caused by the tenacious Turkish defence of Plevna, soon began to hound the South Western Railway.

The alleged failures of railway transport in this campaign were examined by a post-war commission, which noted the difficulties caused to the South Western Railway by the failure of other railways to send enough of their spare locomotives to help out during the crisis. Plans had, in fact, been made for the anticipated wartime traffic, but a locomotive shortage, not of the company's making, had rendered the schedules inoperable. The many variations of locomotive designs used on the Russian railways was a major set-back for the hard-pressed South Western Railway, which could only make use of locomotives which were familiar to that company's staff and for which spare parts were held. Thus an important consequence of this war was the adoption of a government standard locomotive, built nominally for the 'government reserve'; several hundred units of this eight-wheeled freight locomotive were built by various Russian firms and allocated to various state and private railways, especially those serving the border areas. In the 1890s a new government standard locomotive design was adopted and more than 9,000 units were built. This type was invaluable both in the First World War and the subsequent Civil War, being shifted around all over Russia in accordance with the military situation.

The South Western Railway began to play a part in military thinking rather like that of the Est Railway in France. It was obviously a potential front-line railway. The Russians had never made any secret of their interest in the military significance of their railways; indeed this frankness was exploited in the exaggerated comments made by the Russophobe press in Britain. All the same, when a Russian guidebook published in 1898 described one of the South Western Railway's branch lines in the following terms, it was hardly surprising that outside commentators began to believe that every Russian railway had some sinister motive:

'. . . this line has no serious economic significance, but can be regarded as the beginning of a new rail route which in the future will progress further to the west, towards the Austrian frontier, and become a new link connecting Russia with the Slavic lands possessed by Austria–Hungary.'

Shortly before, the Minister of War, whose department had long concerned itself with the pattern of new railway construction, wrote to Tsar Alexander III, expressing succinctly the thoughts of all continental war ministers of the late nineteenth century:

'. . . railways are now the strongest and most decisive element of war. Therefore regardless even of financial difficulties, it is exceedingly desirable to make our railway network equal that of our enemies.'

The British, above all, were interested in Russian railway-building prowess, especially after 1880, when the Russians began to build their Trans-Caspian Railway into Central Asia, a line which eventually goaded the British towards a costly and useless expedition into Afghanistan to forestall the conjectured arrival of Russians in Kabul.

Inside Britain, the initiative in coming to terms with wartime demands on railway transport came from engineers. In 1859 W. Bridges Adams, author of *English Pleasure Carriages*, joint inventor of the fishplate connection between rails, and celebrated for much else besides, wrote an article for the magazine *Once a Week*, in which he expressed the opinion of many British engineers:

> 'The beginning of the end is approaching. Wars cannot be carried on without railways, and the railway is emphatically the offspring and tool of civilisation—not to be maintained without civilisation. It is a weapon of defence and not of attack, and is easily rendered useless to an invading enemy.'

This spirit of optimism, this belief that the railway, because it aids the defender more than the attacker, will deter aggressors, was quite widespread, even though it was shortly to be shaken by the Franco–Prussian War. Adams went further, seeing the railway as a weapon which had the additional advantage of being unsuitable for internal oppression: 'This is precisely the kind of arrangement that could never grow into an instrument of tyranny in England, for the maintenance of the rails would depend on the will of the general community.'

In 1865, at the initiative of the Institution of Civil Engineers, the Engineer and Railway Staff Corps was formed. This organization, consisting of about twenty leading railway engineers who were granted the rank of lieutenant-colonel in the Volunteers, later expanded, but was always an officers-only affair. Its majors were general managers of the bigger railway companies and leading railway contractors, while its captains were traffic managers of main lines, and engineers and general managers of minor ones. Its main purpose was to arrange, in peacetime, that the railways, in time of war, could work together, and co-ordinate with the army and navy. Its first exercises were the drawing up of very detailed movement plans for the transport of troops to places on the eastern and southern coasts which were regarded as likely landing sites for an invader. After a few years these exercises were discontinued, for it was realized that with their dense network and abundant rolling stock the railways would not have the slightest difficulty in conveying troops to threatened areas far faster than an enemy could land his own troops.

Not everyone held the Corps in great esteem. When von Weber's book about German railways and the military was translated into English, the London publishers inserted a long introduction about the situation in Britain, and the role of the new Corps:

'Now we confess to being unable to see anything, when soberly viewed, but mischief to come out of this curious military excrescence. . . . We fully comprehend that its functions in time of peace are to wear a uniform and to flaunt feathers at field-days and reviews, and imagine they are taken for field-officers . . . they dare not interfere with the army. . . . They cannot meddle with the railway authorities. . . . What must be the upshot? That *malgré* the silliness of the position they had assumed in peace, most . . . would have good sense enough to hold their tongues and disappear.'

Interestingly enough, when the well-written history of the Corps, *All Rank and No File*, appeared in 1969 its sole colour picture was a frontispiece of a gentleman wearing a full-dress uniform and flaunting feathers. It is indeed hard to see the justification for this Corps' existence in the twentieth century; its role in preparing British railways for the Second World War appears to have been non-existent and the main demand on its exclusive membership was payment of the annual subscription. In the late nineteenth century, however, it did find a function, even though its members assembled only very rarely. Notably, it participated in the setting up in 1897 of the Army Railway Council, the precursor of the Railway Executive Committee that would supervise the British railways in the First World War. The Council consisted of four managers of large railways and two engineers, representing the Corps, together with three Board of Trade Railway Inspectors (traditionally army officers). The Corps was also responsible for making lists of qualified railway-men who could be enlisted in a reserve, who would then be available for call-up in case of need. An identical Corps was organized in Australia, where, in 1911, on the advice of Lord Kitchener, a similar Railway Council was established.

Linked with the Corps was the *de facto* birth in Britain of the first of the British army's railway units. This was the 2nd Cheshire Railway Volunteer Battalion of the early 1880s. It had arisen as an ordinary volunteer unit whose members happened to come from the railway engineering town of Crewe. Known as the 'Crewe Volunteers', the battalion soon became part of the Royal Engineers and some of its members served in the Nile Valley and South African campaigns.

The Nile Valley campaign was one of several in which the British laid supporting military railways. Earlier, against the King of Abyssinia in 1867–68, a line was laid from the coast towards the scene of operations. This line was of twelve miles, and built by the Royal Engineers with equipment sent from India. Chinese labour was used, but the fact that the line was not quite complete by the time the campaign was won was no reflection on the quality of labour; it was the organization which was incompetent. The concept of Indian railways as a base for operations in East Africa and the Middle East would have a long life, but at this early stage it was a good idea that did not work The locomotives supplied from India were those which the railways were most glad to get rid of, small, worn and hardly usable. The rails were a mixture of odds and ends, often of unusual lengths, kinked and threadbare. Moreover, when the rails were sent the authorities in Bombay neglected to despatch the necessary spikes, delaying the start of construction for several weeks. The rolling stock was obsolete, springless, unlubricated and with weak couplings. Moreover all equipment was originally designed for the Indian broad gauge, and was much heavier than was really needed for this line.

From this inauspicious beginning, the army engineers progressed through a succession of military railways, learning appropriate lessons with each enterprise. The Sudan Military Railways, built in connection with the late nineteenth-century campaign against the Dervishes, were an early example of the Royal Engineers' growing competence in railway-building. These lines were begun during the 1884 British expedition to relieve General Gordon, beleaguered in Khartoum. It was decided to extend the existing railway in the Sudan farther along the Nile, so as to ease the passage of the expedition. Built by British and Egyptian soldiers and labourers, with the help of one railway company of the Royal Engineers, the new line was over fifty miles long. When Khartoum fell, the line was still being continued southwards, but it was not long before the British abandoned it and retreated to the Egyptian frontier. Meanwhile a second attempt to bring rail power to bear against the Dervishes had been undertaken with a line from the Red Sea to the Nile, starting at the port of Suakin. Construction had been entrusted to British contractors in the hope of finishing the line quickly, but a railway company of the Royal Engineers, and some railway craftsmen raised by the Engineer and Railway Staff Corps, were sent to help. This division of responsibility meant that the work went ahead amid confusion and recrimination, while attacks by Dervishes resulted in a number of casualties among the workers. Despite an Anglo–Indian protective force, the construction of fortified posts, and the provision of a bullet-proof train for patrolling the line at night, only twenty miles were laid before it was decided to abandon the project.

However, in the next decade, during the campaign leading to the Battle of Omdurman and the capture of Khartoum, the Royal Engineers excelled themselves. Kitchener's army advanced southwards down a freshly laid railway; although the Dervishes had destroyed the fifty miles previously laid, this track was restored and added to for many more miles down the Nile Valley, the construction proceeding even though the line was in heavy use by the army. Eventually, by May 1897, after a year of work, a 216-mile line had been laid. However, when it was decided to continue to Khartoum in order to break the power of the Dervishes once and for all, Kitchener decided that he would prefer a railway passing directly over the Nubian Desert to one following the winding valley of the Nile. This desert line was surveyed by a Royal Engineers party and construction began in May 1897. Two months later 115 miles were ready, and construction temporarily ceased so that troops could be sent along it to capture a town essential both for the southward advance and for the security of the railway-builders. After this town, Abu Hamed, was captured in August, the line was brought into it, thereby reaching the Nile by a direct line of 232 miles, having been built over waterless desert at a rate of one and a quarter miles per day. The Royal Engineers then continued the line south, first to Atbara after the Dervishes had been defeated at the Battle of Atbara, and then, in 1899, to Khartoum. The railway was the essential part of Kitchener's campaign. Indeed, the Anglo–Egyptian troops were often halted to await completion of a further section of line, and the crucial Battle of Omdurman was won by troops carried and supplied by the railway. High construction standards had been adopted, with heavy trains, carrying up to as much as 200 tons, moving at speeds of up to 25 mph.

Military considerations often affected railway-building decisions in the British Empire, although it was rare for them to take clear precedence over commercial requirements. In India, an early proposal for railway construction was actually defeated because of military opposition. However, when the beginnings of an Indian network were laid, the military advantage of rapid shifts of troops was soon realized. The army in India had two purposes, to maintain internal order and to defend the northern frontiers. Usually it was the first which seemed more important; ever since the Indian Mutiny of 1857, administrators had feared a repetition of that rebellion. Station buildings were accordingly designed with a view to defensibility. Typically, they had few windows but plentiful slits in their walls, and were surrounded by wide open spaces. The larger Indian towns had a 'city' station, but also, on the outskirts, a main 'cantonment' station, serving not only the administrative area but also the garrison; this, it was thought, would prevent popular disturbances threatening the rapid embarkation and disembarkation of troops.

The Indian main lines were laid to a broad gauge (5 ft 6 in), but in due course it was realized that secondary lines would be cheaper if built to a narrower gauge. This proposal caused some agitation among the military staff, which felt that break-of-gauge points would delay troop and supply movements. The Commander-in-Chief, India, raised considerable objections when the Indus Valley line, which led from the port of Karachi to the critical North West Frontier, was begun on the metre gauge. Lord Salisbury, the Secretary of State for India, was eventually persuaded to revoke this decision, and those sections of the line already laid were taken up, to be replaced by broad-gauge track. However, in subsequent years the military acquiesced in the building of metre-gauge lines. But the metre gauge itself had been chosen as the secondary line standard on the basis of military requirements. A 2 ft 9 in gauge had been the first choice, but the Indian Army pointed out that such a gauge could not carry horses two abreast, so the larger gauge was adopted. Later, the army accepted an even narrower gauge; on the grounds that a narrow-gauge railway was better than no railway at all, the strategic lines built in the mountainous areas of the North West Frontier were of the 2 ft 6 in standard. Such lines were unlikely to be of much commercial value, so cheapness of construction was a first requirement. But even in the choice of narrow gauge the army had the last word. A gauge of 2 ft 6 in was not much smaller than metre gauge, so the Indian administration would have preferred to adopt the 2 ft gauge, to make the introduction of a third gauge worth while. However, the army was anxious that in emergency these new lines should be able to borrow rolling stock from other railways, and as several of the Indian princes had built 2 ft 6 in gauge lines in their territories the army thought that that gauge should be chosen for the government lines in the frontier region. This decision was approved by the War Office in London, which secured an official decision that henceforth, in the interest of interchangeability, 2 ft 6 in would be the standard narrow gauge throughout the British Empire.

In the North West Frontier region the spate of railway building coincided with Anglo-Russian tension, itself generated largely by Russian construction of the Trans-Caspian line, which in the minds of both the Disraeli and Gladstone administrations was a clear threat to India. Apart from narrow-gauge strategic railways in this region, the British also built a broad-gauge line to the frontier with Afghanistan near Quetta. This line was begun surreptitiously, as the government wished to avoid alerting the Russians as to what was going on. The project was initially described as a 'road improvement scheme', and to maintain this fiction the engineers were not allowed to lay the temporary railway track customarily used to bring up materials: camels had to be used instead. But when the Russians occupied the Central Asian town of Merv all pretence was dropped, and the line was pushed forward as rapidly as possible as the Sind–Pishin State Railway. Passing for over 200 miles through barren, mountainous and often waterless country, inhabited by armed and very hostile tribesmen, the line threaded long gorges and savage defiles, and was regarded at the time as a wonder of engineering. Intense heat, attacks by tribesmen, and outbreaks of cholera, which in one instance killed a fifth of the work force, meant that construction could only be slow. The line was finally opened in 1887, just as Britain and Russia were settling their disputes amicably.

Even this line, as a feat of railway engineering, was surpassed by the Khyber Railway, finished in 1925. British military expeditions into Afghanistan had usually been disastrous, largely because so many troops died on the advance or the retreat through the Khyber Pass. A railway through the Pass was demanded, and a line of twelve miles from Peshawar to the fort at the entrance to the Pass was soon built; construction beyond that was regarded as impossible for many years. The fold of the mountains, presenting very steep, very narrow and very winding gorges, would have been daunting for builders of a narrow-gauge line, and seemed unconquerable for a broad-gauge route. Nevertheless, a Royal Engineers survey party undertook the impossible and produced a brilliant alignment, making use of reversing stations; over the most difficult sections the trains would zigzag their way up and across the almost vertical mountain sides. The twenty-four-mile extension had two high viaducts as well as the reversing station. At the summit, extensive storage sidings for troop trains were provided, and the crossing stations of the single-track line had loops to accommodate 1,000-foot trains. The station buildings were fortified. Like other strategic lines in this region, the Khyber Railway still exists.

An unwritten code of behaviour governed relations with the local Pathans. The territory of the Railway was regarded as inviolable, but any railwayman or passenger who strayed too far risked being murdered and robbed by the locals. For their tolerance of the railway the tribesmen were allowed to travel without tickets and to carry their firearms at stations and on trains. An official who once required a tribesman to buy a ticket was shot the following night.

It was not in India but in South Africa that the British military railway faced its first major test. Most of the lessons learned by the British army in its Boer War campaigns of 1899–1902 had to be unlearned in the First World War, but the experience in military railway operation was an exception; in this the Boer War was truly a dress rehearsal for the World War. In South Africa, although there were several occasions when the railways were mishandled, there was a readiness both to plan ahead and to recognize shortcomings. Railways were, after all, essential for this campaign in view of the great distances between the British bases on the coast and the Boer republics of the interior against which the troops were directed; from Cape Town to the Boer stronghold of Pretoria was more than 1,000 miles.

The British had made preparations before the war started. In the workshops of the Natal Government Railways ambulance trains and armoured trains were prepared, and a railway company of Royal Engineers was despatched from Britain. Mean-

The Natal Government Railway frequently provided open freight cars for troop movements during the Boer War. Here the Royal Irish Fusiliers are embarking in one such train

while, a Department of Military Railways was established under Major Girouard, who earlier had built the Trans-Nubian line in the Sudan. It was the task of Girouard and his staff to act as intermediaries between the army's operational officers and the railway staffs. In practice, this meant deciding priorities between different types of military traffic, protecting railwaymen from interference and pressure from army officers, and ensuring that the natural tendencies of army officers to retain freight cars, to use trains to run errands, and to demand unnecessary services were kept in check.

In the first few weeks of the war, the Boers captured a considerable amount of territory. The retreating British made only half-hearted efforts to destroy their railway facilities, although the Boers had little use for these anyway; being traditionalists, they preferred to fight their wars from ox-wagons. In fact, some of the most effective railway demolition in Boer-occupied territory was by the Boers themselves; having heard exaggerated rumours about the British armoured trains, they sought to protect themselves by cutting their own lines and destroying their own stock.

After the British had recovered from their early setbacks, they endeavoured to use the railways to advance into Boer territory. There was a shortage of rolling stock, and the 3 ft 6 in gauge lines were only single track. But with strict planning and enforcement of priorities, it was possible to provide a service quite adequate for the needs of the army. The Department of Military Railways each day submitted to Kitchener, the Chief-of-Staff, the number of vehicles that could be despatched northwards, and all army departments had to send their transport requirements to Kitchener's staff, which then decided—giving priority to military needs—which requests should be satisfied and which postponed. In general, troops were encouraged to go by road, leaving the railways free to carry their supplies. Lord Roberts's advance to Bloemfontein was an exception; his 20,000 men and 13,000 horses were all conveyed by rail.

When the Boers were pushed back they thoroughly destroyed the railway facilities, giving the first demonstration of the whole-sale use of dynamite against railways. Often, miles of track were put out of action by dynamite charges laid beneath the rail joints. Bridges were wrecked by larger charges, as were loco-motives, watering facilities and stations. The railway companies and fortress companies of the Royal Engineers were insufficient to deal with all this damage, so a railway pioneer regiment, composed mainly of local miners, was formed to do much of the heavy work. Lines taken over in former Boer territory presented more problems for the Department of Military Railways. The latter set up the Imperial Military Railways to operate and repair these lines, but found that few of the former employees were willing to work under the British regime. Men from the army with peacetime railway experience were thereupon sum-moned to help, together with railwaymen from Cape Colony.

Boer guerilla attacks were usually made on the railways at night, so each day at dawn, trackwalkers set out to inspect the line. Repair trains were held ready at suitable points to move to any section where damage was reported, and normally repairs were effected within an hour or two. Later, blockhouses were built along the railway line, and these, together with armoured

(overleaf) *British troops manning an armoured train during the Boer War. The infantry vehicle shown here is a freight car fitted with armoured sides*

train patrols, deterred the guerillas. Nevertheless, the early morning trains were headed by heavy flatcars, pushed ahead of the locomotive to explode possible mines. Most trains also carried machine guns at the front and rear, and sometimes a light quick-firing gun. Locomotive cabs were armoured against small-arms fire.

With the possible exception of the Russian Civil War, the Boer War witnessed the greatest-ever use of armoured trains. The concept had a great attraction, especially to journalists and arm-chair theorists, but in practice it was too inflexible and vulnerable to become a major weapon. The British began the war with ten such trains, but one was destroyed by the Boers on the first night of the war. At first, they were treated almost as a form of cavalry; used instead of cavalry scouts, they sometimes travelled long distances, until it was realized that, unlike cavalry, they had no alternative return route if they were cut off. Several trains sustained damage in making narrow escapes, while one was actually captured. The latter consisted, from front to rear, of a freight car mounting a naval muzzle-loading gun, a car with armoured, loopholed, sides carrying three sections of the Dublin Fusiliers, the engine and tender, two more armoured cars with infantry and a breakdown crew, and a car carrying tools and repair materials. Winston Churchill, in his *London to Ladysmith via Pretoria*, described the discomfiture of this 120-man train:

'Beyond Chieveley a long hill was lined with a row of black spots, showing that our further advance would be disputed. . . . Colonel Long replied by ordering the train to return to Frere . . . on rounding a corner we saw that a hill which commanded the line at a distance of 6000 yards was occupied by the enemy. . . . The long brown rattling serpent with the rifles bristling from its spotted sides crawled closer to the rocky hillock on which the scattered black figures of the enemy showed clearly. Suddenly three wheeled things appeared on the crest, and within a second a bright flash of light. . . . The Boers had opened fire on us. . . . The train leapt forward, ran the gauntlet of the guns, which now filled the air with explos-ions, swung round the curve of the hill, ran down a steep gradient, and dashed into a huge stone which awaited it on the line at a convenient spot. . . . We were not long left in the comparative peace and safety of a railway accident. . . .'

During the war additional armoured trains were built in South African railway workshops, making a total of nineteen, and their use was better defined. They were manned by infantry, artillery and engineer detachments, the Royal Engineers being equipped for the repair of track and light structures and also providing telegraphers and train crew. All the latter were armed, including the two sets of locomotive men; however, the latter were only expected to use their rifles to repel boarders attempting to enter the locomotive cab. The trains' main duties were to patrol the lines to thwart sabotage attempts, to make reconnaissances, to escort certain trains, to protect stations expecting an enemy attack, and, sometimes, to act in co-ordination with advancing troops to guard flanks and to cut off an enemy's line of retreat.

In the first part of the war, the fact that these trains were commanded by army officers caused complications. As Girouard himself later complained:

'Armoured trains were constantly rushing out, against orders of the Traffic department, sometimes without a "line clear" message, and this caused serious delays to traffic. In fact, instead of assisting traffic by preventing the enemy from interrupting it, they caused more interruptions than the enemy themselves.'

Typical of this confusion was the celebrated occasion when a local commander, not wishing to use his cavalry to escort a large herd of cattle being sent on-the-hoof to market, used an armoured train as escort. This train, proceeding at cow's pace, blocked the main line for hours. But it could be claimed that commanders were badly instructed. There could hardly be a more striking example of equivocal orders than Army Order No. 3 of 24 April, 1901: '. . . it must be distinctly understood that Officers Commanding Sections, Lines of Communications, are on no account to look upon armoured trains as conveniences for inspection purposes, but there is no objection to their being used for this purpose, providing it does not interfere with their patrolling duties.'

The Boer War also demonstrated the first use in war of heavy-calibre rail-mounted guns. The possibility of such weapons had long exercised British minds. William Adams, in an article written during the invasion scare of 1859, when hordes of French soldiers were thought to be on the verge of landing on Britain's south coast, suggested that the cheapest and most effective form of coast defence would be guns fitted to eight-wheel railway cars and hauled by locomotives. Operated on existing and future coastal railways, these guns would make the railway into what amounted to a continuous fortress, and one which could be reinforced with extra firepower long before the enemy could land his troops. Nothing was done to put this idea into practice, and in any case that particular invasion scare was short-lived. However, there were further alarms later in the century. The fear of France and her powerful army was a very real one; among other things this was the deciding factor in the rejection of successive proposals for a Channel Tunnel. Sporadic suggestions were made for rail-mounted coastal defences, but nothing positive was done until 1886, when the Indian Army successfully fired a 40-pounder gun mounted on a standard railway car; in this particular demonstration it was established that the weapon could be fired broadside-on without overturning the car. Then, in 1894, a unit of the Sussex Artillery Volunteers found itself without any allotted duties, and discovered at the same time that there was a 40-pounder gun stored nearby. Many members of this unit were employed at the Brighton Works of the London, Brighton & South Coast Railway, and it was not long before that railway's help was enlisted in designing a railway gun carriage for the surplus weapon. The locomotive superintendent further developed the original idea by mounting a turntable on the car, which enabled the gun to be rotated with ease. He also provided armour plating for the front and sides, leaving an aperture through which the gun could be fired. Official trials were made at Newhaven in May 1894. Shots fired at a target one and a half miles distant included some with the gun at right angles to the line. The recoil cylinder with which the car had been provided absorbed the shock so that not only was there no threat to the stability of the car but there was no damage to the track, and the gun could be fired repeatedly without the need for re-aiming.

The guns used in South Africa were a direct development of these trials, using much larger calibres. Two mountings were built in the workshops of the Cape Government Railway, utilizing old locomotive and tender frames. Intended for the siege of Pretoria, the guns were hardly used in that battle because of the early fall of the stronghold. The smaller of the pair, a 6-inch piece, was successfully used at the Battle of Modder River, and although at

A British armoured train used in the Boer War, showing the naval gun mounted in the leading vehicle

the time it was not fired at an angle greater than 16 degrees from the centreline, it was subsequently tried successfully with broadside firing. The second gun, a 9·2-inch weapon, arrived too late to be used; it was, however, a precursor of the heavy rail-mounted guns used in the two world wars.

Not far from the battlefields of the Boer War, the Germans were perfecting their light field railways. For the economic development of their colony of South West Africa, and for its military security, they had laid a system of 2 ft gauge lines of the type designed for the German army. Experience gained with these lines was absorbed in time to be used for the German *Feldbahnen* of the First World War.

The light field railway had its beginnings in France. Paul Décauville, who had been a gunner during the Franco–Prussian War, inherited an agricultural machinery business and sought to enhance its prospects with a new product—2 ft gauge portable railways which could be used on farms. These lines could be laid down and taken up quickly, without the use of special equipment. Various war ministries, which as the decades passed were becoming increasingly adept at beating ploughshares into swords, realized that at last a true battlefield railway had been invented. The French, German and Russian war ministries were among the first to buy them. The track and equipment were usually placed in store, ready to be used in war, the idea being that the lines would be laid and taken up as troops advanced or retreated. The growing destructiveness of war, demanding unprecedented flows of ammunition and producing large numbers of wounded in need of evacuation, seemed to promise a great future for these lines.

Décauville railways were used on a large scale during the acquisition of Morocco by French forces under General Lyautey just prior to the First World War. The Treaty of Algeciras in 1906, which followed a period of tension between France and Germany generated by colonial jealousies, was remarkable in that it was accompanied by an agreement between those powers that whereas neither should build commercial railways in the region,

Décauville 'portable' railways, invented in the 1870s, reached their peak in the First World War. Here an American locomotive and supply train is using such a railway in France in 1918.

The portability of the Décauville railway is well illustrated by this picture showing how Britain's Indian Army could use the system for its North West Frontier operations. The picture comes from the 1916 Décauville catalogue

military railways were acceptable, and were to qualify as military by being narrow gauge. Indeed, when France built a 1,055 mm gauge line in 1911, the German ambassador protested that 60 cm (2 ft) was the only proper gauge for a military line.

The building and operation of field railways was an additional task for the railway troops that had been organized by most of the great powers. Sometimes modelled on the US Construction Corps of the American Civil War, these had usually started as companies, but had then expanded to battalions or regiments. Usually regular railwaymen were recruited, sometimes as full-time soldiers but more often as reservists. Prussia was one of the first states to organize such troops, and by the turn of the century had a complete railway brigade, while Bavaria had a railway battalion. The Prussian railway troops had the benefit of a regular railway line on which to train. This was the forty-four-mile line from Berlin to Juterbog. This carried considerable civilian traffic, both passenger and freight, but was operated by Prussian railway troops, aided by a railway detachment from Saxony. In Austria–

Hungary there was a railway regiment, together with a railway pioneer corps for the labouring work. The Austrian field railways were distinguished by their use of 70 cm as well as 60 cm lines. In France there was a railway regiment as well as several railway pioneer companies. About 400 miles of Décauville track was in store, as well as a range of standard bridge spans for repairing demolished structures. There was no military training railway, but the men were attached for certain periods to the main railways, and there was a company permanently employed on the Etat Railway's main line between Orleans and Chartres. The Russian army was a real pioneer in the use of railway troops, having formed a railway construction brigade in the 1850s to help build the St Petersburg–Warsaw railway. The first railway-operating battalion had been organized in the Russo–Turkish War and by the end of the century much experience had been gained during the army's construction of the Trans-Caspian Railway. Britain and America were much less advanced, relying on recruiting railwaymen in emergencies. However, in more recent times both Britain and the USA built short railways for the sole purpose of training railway troops and the last sizeable training railways to survive after the Second World War, at least in the west, were the Longmoor Military Railway in Britain and the Fort Eustis line in the USA.

The railway age was also the age of colonization, so it was natural that the new technology should be applied in the newly acquired lands. In this application the distinction between railways of commercial and military significance is even more blurred than in continental Europe. The great transcontinentals certainly had a military potential which was quite clearly spelled out at the time. Even the first American transcontinental, the Union Pacific–Central Pacific link, was approved largely because some congressmen regarded it as necessary for national defence. In the 1862 debate in the House of Representatives, a representative from California made his thoughts quite clear, 'We must have a railroad across the continent by which troops and munitions of war can be rapidly transported to that coast.' And a fellow representative put the concept into different words: 'In case of foreign war you cannot hold this continent together without rapid communication across it.'

The Canadian Pacific, too, was largely conceived as a line of military value. In this case, the motivation was the possibility of moving troops from eastern Canada to the west, in order to counter possible incursions northwards by either the armies or the armed citizens of the USA. At that time, though, the British were already sufficiently diplomatic to avoid mentioning this aspect more frequently than was necessary to raise support for the railway, preferring to emphasize a desire to integrate the British Columbians more fully into Canada as a whole. The rather difficult route of the line through the Kicking Horse Pass was chosen by the government largely because the easier alternative alignment passed vulnerably close to the US frontier. As it happened, the Canadian Pacific was used for a very important military purpose when it was only partly completed. The second Riel Rebellion burst out in the prairies in 1885, and troops were urgently needed in the Winnipeg district. Van Horne, the General Manager of the Canadian Pacific, had gained experience of troop movements during the American Civil War and, mindful of the lessons taught by that war, offered to send troops from Ottawa in eleven days, provided he had a free hand with no official interference. In fact the first troops to be despatched arrived after only a few days, having, despite the Canadian winter, travelled on flatcars over completed sections and been sledged over the several uncompleted sections. Later in this campaign a troop train carrying the Montreal Light Infantry became the first through train to run to Winnipeg, having been held up *en route* to enable the final spikes to be driven; at untested bridges the troops detrained, marched over, and were rejoined by their train on the other side.

It was not until the Second World War that the first US transcontinental really played a strategic role; in that conflict it was one of several transcontinentals used for transferring troops and munitions to the Pacific war zone. But since it was, early in its life, an instrument for the spreading of settlers, often by force, into lands previously occupied by Indians, it could be regarded as a colonizing railway. Such internal colonization was also a feature of the Russian Empire, which in the nineteenth century was spreading eastwards and south-eastwards. Early Russian railways, frankly described as military and built by soldiers, included a line across the Caucasus and, later, the Trans-Caspian Railway. Both these railways were intended to facilitate the subjugation of local tribes and peoples who were resisting Russian encroachments. However, the Trans-Caspian Railway, built across desert from the eastern shore of the Caspian into Central Asia, was a cause of great alarm in London, for each mile completed seemed to bring it closer to the Indian frontier. In fact this railway was never used to support an attack on British India, but it admirably fulfilled its original purpose of violent colonization, and later became an important part of the economic development of Russian Central Asia.

But although it was the Trans-Caspian that caused most anxiety in London, it was the Trans-Siberian project that captured the world's imagination and caused the greatest anxiety in Tokyo, Peking and Washington. This railway, apart from being a means to develop Siberia, had an explicitly colonizing and military purpose. Russian administration had reached the Pacific at Vladivostok in 1860, and St Petersburg, like other capitals, was looking to the weak Chinese Empire as a field for extending its strategic and commercial influence. Eastern Siberia was geographically too unpromising to justify an expensive railway, so although it could be claimed that the line was worth while for economic reasons in western and central Siberia, the eastern section had a quite uncommercial justification. The needs of the navy, which had a potentially well-sited base at Vladivostok that could only be partially exploited without a rail link with European Russia, and the needs of the War Ministry, which did not regard enthusiastically the prospect of passing reinforcements to the Far East through the Suez Canal and the Japanese-dominated straits, were the inducements taking the line through to the Pacific.

Profiting from the weakness of the Chinese government, the Russians secured a concession enabling them to build the eastern part of their new railway across Manchuria, nominally part of the Chinese Empire. This not only shortened the distance to Vladivostok but also took a Russian railway into Chinese territory, which seemed to offer great commercial and military advantages. To make the agreement more palatable, the section through China was built, owned and managed by a private company, the Chinese Eastern Railway. This had its head office in Paris, but in reality it was completely controlled by the Russian Ministry of Finance. To protect this railway the Company was allowed to station so-called railway guards in a belt of territory along its length; these were former members of the Tsarist army, including some who had served in crack Cossack regiments. They probably enjoyed their status because, being employed by the Ministry of

Finance, they received much higher pay than they had when under the War Ministry.

One of the most emotional issues which drove the Chinese to the Boxer Rebellion in 1900 was the question of railway concessions granted to foreign companies by the Chinese government. The secret association, the Society of Harmonious Fists, could base its appeal both on the Chinese distrust of foreigners and the dislike of railways. When the foreign legations were besieged in Pekin and the European powers despatched relief forces, the Russians were able to arrive quickly, as their troops could move most of the way by railway. In the meantime the Russians had been fighting a virtual full-scale war in defence of their Chinese Eastern Railway, one of the most popular targets for the insurgents. The rebellious Chinese army caused great damage to the line by shellfire, and Russian station staff and their families were sometimes murdered. However, the growing Russian railway town at Kharbin, deep in Manchuria, survived. The railway guards fought very well; when they took Chinese prisoners they sent them west, to work on building the Transbaikal section of the Trans-Siberian Railway.

After the defeat of the Boxers the Chinese Eastern Railway was rehabilitated. It had already become the basis for a further move into the Chinese Empire, with a line (the South Manchuria Railway) laid south from Kharbin to connect with the two ports of Dalny and Port Arthur, which had been leased by Russia. Port Arthur had been a former Chinese naval base and the Russian government, with the aid of the new railway link, transformed it into a large fortified naval and military stronghold.

The emergence of Russia, with its new transcontinental railway, as a Pacific power was not welcomed by other governments, which had their own ambitions in the area. The Americans were mainly worried about the effect on trade, but the Japanese were also anxious on strategic grounds. The militarization of Japan had been proceeding rapidly in previous decades. China had been soundly beaten in a recent war, and the Japanese people were expecting their government to win further great victories and gain more commercial booty. A Russian fleet at Port Arthur, a Russian commercial port at Dalny and the Russian railway network seemed to threaten all these hopes. The most sensitive region was Korea, where both the powers had ambitions. When the Japanese obtained a concession to build a railway to Seoul, the Korean capital, the Russians were very agitated, but this agitation was passed to the Japanese when a French company building a railway north from Seoul was persuaded to use the Russian 5 ft gauge and thereby make feasible a possible through route right from Russia into Korea. From 1902 there was a state of tension between Russia and Japan until, in February 1904, the Japanese launched a surprise attack on Port Arthur and thereby started the Russo–Japanese War.

This war, the first of the modern wars of mass destruction, was further distinguished in that it was very largely a railway war; indeed, the building of the Trans-Siberian Railway to the Pacific may be regarded as the fundamental cause of hostilities. The choice of February 1904 for the beginning of the war was made for two reasons; later in 1904 the Russian naval squadron was to be reinforced by new ships sent from the Baltic, and in February 1904 the Trans-Siberian Railway still had a very limited traffic capacity. Not only were there too few passing loops provided for this single-track line, but one difficult section around Lake Baikal was not complete; troops and their supplies would have to cross the lake by ferry in summer and on foot across the ice in

Russian officers, en route to the Russo-Japanese War in 1904, pose in front of their train on the Trans-Siberian Railway

winter. Although declarations by defeated generals have to be read with caution, the claim by the Russian commander, Kuropatkin, that he could have won the war if the Trans-Siberian had been able to pass more trains, seems to be quite justified. After all, the Japanese relied precisely on this factor when they decided to attack. Japanese optimism about the Trans-Siberian's incapacity was fed by the Japanese military attaché in St Petersburg, Colonel Tanaka Giichi. Tanaka hated Russians and badly wanted war, so he sent to his superiors deliberately falsified estimates of the railway's lack of traffic capacity. Obviously Tanaka was a man with a great future; he became Japanese prime minister in the 1920s.

The land war was fought in Manchuria. Having won command of the sea, the Japanese were able to send their entire army to fight, whereas the very much larger Russian army was stationed in Europe, and could be sent only slowly to the Far East. This meant that all the initial battles were won by the Japanese, and by the time an overwhelming force of more than a million men had been moved east by the Tsarist government the Russian people had had enough of successive defeats; the 1905 rebellion forced Russia to accept defeat just as she was poised for victory.

In these circumstances it was only natural to blame the Trans-Siberian Railway. But in reality the management of this line did very well. That management, in effect, included the Minister of Transport, Prince Khilkov. Khilkov was a keen student of American railway practice, and had once worked in a British locomotive factory. He took a personal interest in improving the Trans-Siberian line and might have achieved more than he did if the army could have provided a similarly intelligent person to direct military traffic. As it was, military supplies were despatched without reference to the ability of the railway to pass them or of the recipients to unload them. Until late 1904 the line remained broken at Lake Baikal. When the lake first froze troops marched across, with their baggage and supplies moving by sledge. When the winter really set in a railway track was laid across the lake. This line could not take the weight of locomotives, and was sometimes disturbed by weak ice and earth tremors. Freight cars were sent across in ones and twos, hauled by horses. However, the great need of the Chinese Eastern Railway for locomotives was satisfied by dismantling engines, despatching them across the ice railway, and reassembling them on the other shore.

*The railway laid by the Russians across the ice of Lake Baikal in 1904
could not bear the weight of locomotives, so freight cars were hauled across
individually by horses*

After the track around Lake Baikal had been laid the line was
still overloaded, because the main bottleneck had not been the
lake but the Chinese Eastern Railway. At one period all movement into the junction at Kharbin had to be prohibited, to give
time to sort out the utter congestion of the railway lines at this
point. Meanwhile, throughout the length of the railway, extra
passing loops were built. Whereas at the beginning of the war the
Russians expected to operate only three pairs of trains daily, this
capacity was progressively increased so that by the end of the war
sixteen pairs were handled. Apart from the additional loops,
better traffic control contributed to this achievement; trains were
scheduled to move slowly, but at a standard speed. Locomotives
and rolling stock were transferred from other railways, and in key
places bridges and track were strengthened. To prevent further
congestion on the Chinese Eastern Railway, the eastern part of
the route was placed under martial law. This enabled military
courts to treat as deserters any railwaymen who refused to work
long hours (some railwaymen at some periods were required to
work several days without a break, a practice which, because of
increasing accident-proneness, became self-defeating). In general,
the military committed the faults which any observer of the

American Civil War might have anticipated. But the Russian command did introduce one new example of transport mis-management, the widespread use of special trains for important personages. At times railway traffic was held up for hours by these trains. A British attaché made some acid comments, later printed by the War Office, about the Russian Viceroy of the Far East, Admiral Alexeiev:

'The chief of the Viceroy's Staff was the intermediary between Admiral Alexeiev and General Kuropatkin, the former being at Mukden and the latter at Liao-yang, thirty-seven miles distant. Frequent conferences took place between Kuropatkin and this officer, who always used to come in a special train to Liao-yang. This necessitated the line being kept clear for indefinite periods of time and dislocated all the other traffic arrangements, as the then chief of the railways himself declared.

'In the first days of May 1904, the Viceroy and the Grand Duke Boris were at Port Arthur, and wished to leave it before they should be cut off. I heard that they actually took three special trains to quit Port Arthur, namely, one for each of them, and one for their baggage and stores. This entirely upset the troop train, supply, and ammunition services. . . .'

Because much of the food required by the Russian troops could be acquired locally, most of the line capacity was devoted to troop and ambulance trains. The latter ran from the base hospitals to European Russia, often terminating their journey at Moscow and St Petersburg, but not before dropping off many of their wounded at intermediate towns. The troop trains typically consisted of two eight-wheel 'government reserve' locomotives hauling twenty-eight troop-carrying freight cars; that is, ordinary freight cars provided with windows, a stove and sleeping shelves. Six additional freight cars were provided for kit and ammunition, and there was a conventional passenger car for the officers. Such a train carried 1,064 men and thirty-six officers. Transit time from Europe was sometimes as long as fifty days, although this included frequent rest stops. The prolonged separation of the officers from their men on these trains was later said to have facilitated the spread of subversive propaganda, since soldiers were free to while away the hours listening to the talk of discontented reservists.

Both sides made great use of Décauville narrow-gauge field rail-ways, especially towards the end of the war, when the campaign became static. The longest was probably a Russian line laid near Mukden. This was of thirty miles, and its horse-drawn wagons took only about six hours, in favourable conditions, to cover that distance. The wagons could carry one and three-quarter-ton loads, or could be fitted to accommodate eight stretchers; this method of conveying front-line wounded was regarded both by the medical service and by the victims as the most comfortable. Earlier, as the Japanese advanced northwards away from the sea, they faced a communications problem that was only partially solved by the import of coolies and the issue of thousands of handcarts. But three of the Japanese armies were soon able to make use of rail transport, based on the Russian-built South Manchurian Railway. In some areas narrow-gauge lines were laid from the main line to serve army bases, while the main stem of the Railway, from Port Arthur northwards, was utilized with improvised methods. The Russians had removed loco-motives, but the track was mainly intact. Russian freight cars, nominally of twenty-ton capacity, but loaded by the Japanese only up to five tons, were hauled along the line by teams of sixteen coolies (eight pushing and eight pulling on ropes). Soon several such cars were operated as one train. A forty-car train seems to have been the record, but after some disastrous if spectacular runaways down gradients, amid a scurry of entangled coolies, a ten-car limit was imposed. Eventually, this line was converted to the Japanese 3 ft 6 in gauge, with locomotives and rolling stock provided by the Japanese railways.

This war witnessed the occasional use of railways on the battlefield itself. The Russians, as they retreated northwards along the line of the South Manchurian Railway, used to the full the benefit of interior lines of communication. Trains brought their men to the battlefield, and sometimes took them away after defeat. In the last big battle of the war, Mukden, it was when Japanese cavalry threatened to cut the railway behind the Russians that the latter began their retreat. At one of the earlier battles, at Telissu, the Japanese advanced the timing of their attack when they noticed that trains were arriving from the north, loaded with Russian reinforcements. During that engagement more trains arrived on the battlefield with fresh troops, who conducted a holding operation while the trains went back with wounded and weary troops. When the rearguard subsequently withdrew, covered by Russian cavalry, the Japanese could not pursue their beaten enemy. They were unable to use the railway, and their Chinese coolies and carters refused to work as it was a Chinese holiday.

Western newspaper readers, who were far better informed about the war than the Russians or Japanese, found the Great Train Chase of this war especially exciting. This, pitting horses against the steam locomotive, was won by the latter. It happened during a big Russian cavalry sweep behind the Japanese lines. Aimed at

A Russian idea for patrolling railway lines in the Russo-Japanese War. This device did not, however, gain the ready acceptance anticipated by its inventor

the Japanese supply base of Yinkou and its railway link, its first achievement was the cutting of the main railway and telegraph line. However, the Russian cavalry had apparently received no instruction in the subject of railway demolition. The Japanese restored services within six hours, which was about the same time as the Russians took to do their damage. A Russian detachment was then sent to destroy Yinkou's rail link, while the main body, thereby protected from Japanese reinforcements, moved against the town itself. The demolition detachment did manage to cut the line, but only after allowing a Japanese train to pass. So the main Russian body found itself overtaken by a trainload of Japanese reinforcements. As the Japanese infantry, from the train windows, watched the Russians hurrying along on a parallel course, the locomotive slowly drew ahead, and by the time the Russians arrived at Yinkou the Japanese were disembarked and occupying defensive positions. The frustrated Russians fired a few shots and then retired.

The Russo–Japanese War, although it certainly emphasized the importance of railway transport, was so unique that it hardly offered any useful experience to the military planners of the various European powers. The German Great General Staff, which more than most other staffs was convinced that a large-scale European war was inevitable, rightly felt that its own railway plans were too sophisticated to benefit from the lessons of this war except in the matter of light field railways.

Ever since the 1864 war against Denmark, the Prussian, and later the imperial, military staff officers worked out increasingly detailed plans for the use of railways in wartime. Profiting, though not always, from the lessons of the various wars, and especially of the Franco–Prussian War, it was found expedient to issue instructions for almost every eventuality and for almost every possible requirement; rules were even laid down about the proper accommodation to be provided for carrier pigeons on the troop trains. Eventually, at the turn of the century, the accretion of so many regulations and modifications of regulations threatened to defeat the whole purpose of the organization as officers floundered among the mass of documents. Thus with a new edition of the field service regulations an effort was made to simplify the procedures laid down for the railways. Even then, however, the German railway war plans were worked out in greater detail than those of other countries.

In the last pre-war decade the strategic situation of Germany, lying between a hostile Russia and a hostile France, virtually guaranteed that transport would be the key element, at least in the early stages of the anticipated war. Although the German population and industrial resources considerably exceeded those of France, the higher French conscription rate and the enormous army of tsarist Russia more than redressed the balance. For Germany to survive there seemed only one viable strategy, to make an immediate attack on France with overwhelming force, so as to win a crushing victory within six weeks and then redeploy the German forces eastwards to meet the Russians. The latter were expected to mobilize much slower than the Germans, because of the greater distances and the thinner railway network. In fact, it was on this slow Russian mobilization that the German strategy depended. In the decade before 1914 the German strategy was embodied in the Schlieffen Plan which, though modified from time to time, retained its essential element of an initial attack consisting of a wheeling movement by the German armies, with their northernmost forces advancing almost to the English Channel before turning south towards Paris. Whereas, therefore, the southernmost German units would merely advance directly westwards against Paris, the northern wing would have a much greater distance to travel, and for this reason a shortcut across Belgium was envisaged. Although this feature of an attack through Belgium was only half-expected by the staffs of the French and British armies, the general strategy was fully anticipated; one of several indications of German planning was the pattern of railway-building on the German side of the frontier in the pre-war years.

It is doubtful whether the Schlieffen Plan could have succeeded, for logistical reasons. Because the French were expected to destroy their railways as they retreated, the Germans relied on rail transport for troop movement only as far as the frontier. From there the soldiers would march to Paris. It was expected, however, that rail transport would be restored soon enough to pass supplies to the troops. In theory and in practice this was an over-optimistic assumption.

But despite its defects, which were quite obvious to Schlieffen's successor, the younger von Moltke, the Plan was Germany's only chance, once she had become embroiled in a two-front war. The Russian and the French staffs were quite aware of the German dilemma, and came to the same conclusion. For them, therefore, peacetime planning was a question of finding ways to oppose the German strategy. The building of new railways towards and behind the frontiers was one policy, while the continual improvement of the mobilization plans was another.

The German staff had at its disposal in 1914 all the railways which it needed. From the army corps mobilization centres in the interior, there were thirteen lines leading to the frontier deployment areas in the west. The 8th Army, destined to deploy on the eastern front, had three lines, of which two were double track. Four double-track routes had been assigned for connecting the western and eastern fronts. Behind the western front were four double-track lines running parallel to the front, by which it was possible to send four army corps from Cologne to Strasbourg in just three hours. All these lines, while carrying ordinary commercial traffic in the years before the war, had been strengthened to carry heavier locomotives.

The German staff had a strong and permanent influence in pre-war railway policy. Indeed, it was military objections to electrification on grounds of vulnerability that prevented the Prussian State Railways electrifying lines near the frontier as well as routes which were regarded as military main lines; even those sections which were electrified had to be equipped for a return of steam traction in case of war. The General Staff had a railway section which involved itself in all aspects of railway policy; notably it had a great influence on plans for new railway construction, on standardization policies and on the technical level of lines of military significance. The question of standardization was especially important. The German railways were divided into tne railways of the various states and, although the Prussian State Railway was by far the largest, systems such as those of Bavaria and Saxony were sufficiently large to present problems, in the 1870–71 war, to the through running of trains and to the transfer of rolling stock from one railway to another in wartime. The Railway Section of the General Staff was one of several influences which persuaded the different railway administrations to adopt Prussian standards. One technical feature originating on the Prussian railways was the two-piece locomotive chimney. Having had so many chimneys knocked off by French bridges during the Franco–Prussian War, the locomotive department introduced a detachable top section for its chimneys. At a certain sacrifice in terms of draught for the fire, such locomotives could operate abroad with only the lower section of their chimneys. Thus was born the gibe that German locomotives were designed to fit the clearances of other countries' railways. Interestingly, the new locomotives designed in the 1920s retained this feature.

At the lower levels, military needs were looked after by the line *Kommandanturs*. A *Kommandantur* was established for each railway management area and consisted of an officer of the general staff and a high official of the local management. In wartime the *Kommandantur* became all-powerful in its locality and it was a promising means of co-ordinating military and railway interests, that problem which was fundamental to wartime railway operation. Its constant contact with the commanders of military units based in its locality served the same purpose. Apart from the *Kommandanturs* established in the separate management regions of the railways, each railway had a member for military affairs on its administration. This member, while maintaining contact with the *Kommandanturs* of his railway, was also responsible for the technical preparation of the railway for wartime demands; the strengthening of the track, the building of sidings and crossing places, provision of loading and unloading platforms, reception or despatch of transferred locomotives and rolling stock, provision of feeding and watering points, preparations for converting freight cars for troop carrying, and plans for maintaining or cancelling ordinary trains in emergencies. So wide and important were his duties that each year his work was subject to inspection by a commission consisting of the chief of the Railway Section of the General Staff and a high official of the railway.

The German mobilization plan was redrawn each year, so as to take into account changing military priorities and changing railway facilities. An initial conference was held in January between the Railway Section and the operations planning staff of the army. This was followed in mid-February by a conference in which the problems raised in the first conference were settled. From this there emerged a traffic plan for each of the main lines destined for military use; these documents were highly confidential and their major purpose was to enable corps commanders to determine how long it would take for their various units to be fully mobilized. The preparation of traffic plans was not especially difficult, except for those of the first and second day of mobilization, where the regularity of movement was all-important; the plans for these two days were worked out by the Railway Section of the Staff.

Transfers of personnel and rolling stock were included in the plan, so as to enable the less affected railways to help the others. In 1914 it was planned that of the twenty-six railway directorates, nine (Cologne, Saarbrucken, Ludwigshafen, Kassel, Bromberg, Poznan, Königsberg, Breslau and Berlin) would need to receive 530 locomotives and 8,650 freight cars. These were to be transferred in the first four days of mobilization.

The plan for deployment, as distinct from that for the mobilization, was worked out somewhat differently. In the final months of the current mobilization year the chief of the Great General Staff transmitted to the Railway Section the changes in deployment intentions for the coming year. After studying this, and sometimes making suggestions, the Railway Section, consulting with the operations planners, drew up the traffic plan for deployment, making use of any improvements in the railways' potential carrying capacity that had been made in the previous year. Briefly, the deployment plan was based on three categories of traffic. First came the frontier defence troops, whose movement began not with the declaration of mobilization but earlier, on the reception of a message stating that there was a threat of war. Evacuation from threatened areas could also be included in this category. There were no timetables prepared for this category; the movement would start after an order from the Railway Section and the scheduling would be the business of railway administrations, on the demand of the *Kommandanturs*. However, to ensure that these urgent movements would proceed smoothly, the local railway directorates received in peace-time brief summaries of what would be required, so that they would be able to bring the necessary rolling stock to the loading platforms in good time. In the second category came the covering troops, intended to protect the regions of deployment from enemy interference. These troops would be ready for movement as soon as mobilization was declared, or at least within a couple of days of the declaration. With them would also travel units of railway troops, which would make the arrangements for unloading the third category of traffic, the main body of the armies, intended for the strategic deployment. This would begin to move from the evening of the fifth day of mobilization, the second-category traffic occupying the first four days.

Apart from its great bulk, what distinguished the third category movement was its regularity. Consisting of large standard-size units moving between a limited number of embarkation and dis-embarkation points, it was the kind of traffic for which railway transport was ideal. Its handling was not therefore quite as formidable an undertaking as the statistics suggested. Each rail-way deployment route had a standard capacity fixed at 50/24 (that is, fifty pairs of trains each twenty-four hours), although in exceptional cases this could be raised to 60/24. As some confusion and mishaps were regarded as inevitable, each day a four-hour pause was scheduled, which would enable problems to be sorted out, delayed trains to regain their place in the timetable, and unplanned entire trains to find a path. A corps of the active army was to be provided with 140 trains, and a reserve corps with eighty-five. Cavalry divisions were allocated thirty-one trains each. To allow for loading time, each corps was allocated twenty trains each day, so that it would take a week to entrain. At the divisional level this meant one train every two hours, a rate which would enable one division to use one loading platform. The first trains were reserved for essential administrative staff needed at the disembarkation point, pioneer units and field bakeries, followed by cavalry and then the infantry and the infantry artillery. The heavy artillery and its carts moved away last.

The railways were well provided with loading and unloading platforms of the same length as the standard military train. Small stations had unloading bays for artillery and supply carts. At most stations a hard-surfaced road was laid alongside the outer track, and in emergencies could be used as an unloading square. A trainload of infantry was allowed one hour to entrain or detrain, although the men themselves were allowed only fifteen minutes, and the horses twenty. An artillery battery was allowed two hours. Meal stops lasted three-quarters of an hour or one hour, and soldiers were allotted up to twenty minutes for buying local produce from station pedlars. Some practice had been obtained in the successive summer manoeuvres, where an effort was made to include a rapid and intensive troop movement by rail.

All the essential data was incorporated into two series of docu-ments. Traffic movement orders were issued for each line of the deployment for the use of the railway administrations, while traffic plans and timetables were issued only to the higher military authorities. The traffic movement orders were printed for the first four days of mobilization, and in only very small numbers to ensure secrecy. The orders for the later days of mobilization were to be printed only after mobilization was declared. In any case, corps commanders received these documents only after the declaration, again for reasons of secrecy. However, for the first four days of mobilization they did receive enough information to enable them to make essential preparations for their movement. Contingency plans also existed to cope with serious accidents resulting in line blockage. These plans, however, do not appear to have been distributed to anybody outside the General Staff. In 1913, owing to increasing complexity and to an appreciation of political realities, the practice ceased of composing two plans, one for war against Russia only and another for a war in which the main armies would be sent to the western front. At the same time, efforts were made to make the plan more flexible. War games were held, sometimes called 'railway manoeuvres', in which staff officers were confronted with situations requiring rapid reformulation of transport plans: a line was suddenly declared blocked, or a radical change made in deployment plans.

In 1913 efforts were made to plan the so-called 'economic traffic'. This consisted of civilian necessities, mainly fuel, food and materials for the industrial towns. In principle, during the mobilization period civilian traffic was to cease, but it was feared that this might be impracticable. The military, transport and city authorities therefore organized themselves into 'economic mobilization commissions' to evolve methods of reducing as far as possible civilian demands on transport. The accumulation of local stocks was the first and most obvious of their initiatives. However, it was realized that this might not be enough, and railway managements were therefore authorized, on certain lines, to run trains of livestock, milk and other foodstuffs during the mobilization period.

The French mobilization and deployment plans were almost as thorough as the German. Indeed, every year staff officers from the General Staff's 4th Section (which dealt with transport), as well as younger officers fresh from courses, would visit traffic centres in eastern France to acquaint themselves with the facilities and layout. The Est Railway, which served the region separating Germany from Paris, had a special relationship with the government, which provided funds for double-tracking, signalling and loops which would not have been justified by purely commercial considerations. The Austro-Hungarian Empire also had its plans, modelled on the German, but they were rather more complex because the Viennese military authorities faced many more possible combinations of enemies; in the event, despite assertions that the Austrian bureaucracy could do nothing right, the Empire's railways carried out their military role quite effectively in 1914. The British were far less concerned than the continental powers about railborne mobilizations. However, there were occasional exercises to test how fast troops could be deployed to meet invasion threats. The army manoeuvres of 1912 were especially noteworthy in this respect, with large bodies of troops being despatched to East Anglia. King George V, who attended, made complimentary remarks about the railways' competence in shifting troops, and the magazine *Punch* also seems to have been very satisfied:

> 'A feature of the manoeuvres which has given widespread satisfaction is the demonstration that a rapid concentration of troops by rail is possible without dislocation of the ordinary civil traffic. One of the chief objections to hostilities in this country disappears now that it has been shown that our golfers would be able to get to their courses without interference.'

In the summer of 1914, however, it was the Russian mobilization plans that were the key to political and strategic thinking. This was partly because the war originated as a quarrel between Russia, firmly in alliance with France, and Austria, which was allied with Germany. And partly it was because Germany's strategy, indeed her survival in a two-front war, depended on the anticipated Russian tardiness in mobilizing and deploying her forces. When Count Schlieffen drew up his plan he calculated, on good information, that Russia could send only about 200 military trains to the front daily (compared, for example, with the 650 trains that Schlieffen envisaged sending against France through Cologne alone). It was on this basis that Schlieffen allowed himself six weeks to defeat France before redeploying his main forces to the Eastern Front. But after 1910 the tsarist government, while allocating funds for military expansion, spent additional money on improving the railways serving the frontier. By 1914, about 360 trains could be despatched to the front each day. Moreover, after 1912 an increasing proportion of the Russian active army was permanently stationed in Poland, considerably easing the transport problem, and in the same year a new concept was introduced, a statutory 'period of preparation for war', which provided an intermediate stage between peace and general mobilization. Russia knew that her mobilization would be equivalent to a declaration of war, given the German need to be quick on the draw, and the new intermediate period was St Petersburg's version of the concept of 'graduated response'. In this period there would be a very limited call-up of reserves, and the railways would be enabled to start their preparations. The so-called Russian 'Big Programme' covering the years 1914 to 1917 was the climax of these moves. This not only envisaged more military expenditure but, again, considerable railway investment.

The French government guaranteed Russian railway loans raised in France, and French military advisers made suggestions about railway-building and railway improvement; the French had an urgent need for an effective Russian army to take the anticipated German pressure off their own forces. Money was spent on building new lines to the frontier and parallel to the frontier, on providing new sidings, loading and unloading platforms and, above all, better signalling. The long Russian lines were usually equipped with the cheapest forms of train control, which considerably limited their capacity; there was little of the block signalling apparatus used at that time on western railways.

The result of all these measures was that the Russian General Staff, looking forward to 1917, could envisage passing 560 daily trains to the frontier. With the measures taken in 1912, this meant that the Russian mobilization would take only three days longer than the German, assuming that the Germans could make no further improvements in their own plans. Not only this, but already in 1914 it was clear that Russian deficiencies could no longer be relied on to make the Schlieffen Plan work. The Russian mobilization plan due to be introduced in September 1914 envisaged the mobilization of two-thirds of the army in eighteen days, again just three days longer than the period required by the Germans to mobilize all their forces.

But the Russian army was almost three times larger than the German. For the German General Staff, which was well aware of what was happening in Russia, it was ominously clear that if Germany was to fight a war on two fronts, and any other kind of war was unlikely, 1914 might well be the last possible year in which to do so. And even then the Schlieffen Plan would be a close-run thing. Those who, after 1914, claimed to have forecast that Germany would go to war after the 1914 harvest on the basis that by then the Kiel Canal would have been widened, may have got the right answer but did so for the wrong reasons. Germany's now-or-never recourse to war had little to do with the ability to move Dread-noughts between the Baltic and the North Sea. But it may have had something to do with the state of Russia's railways. When the war did break out, the German Staff was in the middle of a desperate project designed to speed deployment by a doubling of average train speeds.

The Russian mobilization plans were revised less frequently than those of the Germans; possibly the Russian army felt that it had insufficient intellectually qualified officers to spare for the very intricate labour required for an annual revision. Plan No. 19, which was applied in August 1914, had been compiled in 1910, and did not reflect the great improvements in railway facilities achieved since then, This fact, plus the inclusion in Plan 19 of various hidden reserves, probably the work of railway officials who thought it best in 1910 not to reveal the maximum of which the railways were capable, meant that the Russian mobilization went very smoothly, and in some cases faster than planned. There were two variants, 19G envisaged a war in which Germany would be the main enemy, and 19A was to cope with a situation in which Austria was the main enemy. But both plans assumed that Austria and Germany would be in alliance. The plans covered the two weeks after the Tsar's declaration of mobiliza-tion. As with the German plan, no attempt was made to forecast the following weeks. Each railway received the sections of the plan which concerned its own duties, but did not open the sealed package, which was placed in an iron box until mobilization. However, some key railway staff were allowed brief details, in order that they should be better prepared when the time came. It was expected that almost all commercial traffic would cease during mobilization, even on the lines not directly affected. The curtailment of traffic on these lines would enable them to con-centrate on despatching locomotives, rolling stock and key personnel to the lines serving the frontiers. It was anticipated that only one civilian service, a mail train, would operate on each line, leaving plenty of capacity for the military trains. The latter would move at 400 kilometres (250 miles) per day, stopping only to water the horses or for the occasional hot meal, and for engine-changing. On the double-track routes equipped with better signalling a line capacity of 36/24 was the norm.

The first three or four days of mobilization were not expected to witness very heavy traffic. In those days the transfers of rolling stock would take place, care being taken to avoid sending oil-burning locomotives to areas where coal and wood fuels were the norm. Freight cars would be unloaded and made available to the military. Many of them would be converted to troop-carrying use; the inscription '40 men 8 horses' was as common on the Russian as on the French railways. By the fifteenth day after the declaration half of the infantry would be mobilized, and three-quarters by the twentieth. The railways in Russian Poland, ex-pected to be closest to the fighting, were given five days, and other railways up to eleven days, in which to reach full mobilization readiness. These allowances were rather generous and meant that units might be mobilized several days before the railways could receive them.

With each of the great continental powers considering its mobilization plan the key to survival in a major war, no threat to its execution could be tolerated. The tsarist government, anticipat-ing that the tense period before a war would be the time chosen by strikers, and perhaps revolutionaries, to exert their pressure, made its own secret plans to cope with this possibility. The secret police, through selected army officers and railway officials, arranged for peace-keeping armoured trains that would cruise along lines affected by strikes and civil disorders. These trains would disperse insurgents with their troops, repair damaged installations with their staff of railway maintenance men, restore communications with their telegraph contingent, and make deserved or demonstrative arrests with their police section. In the event these trains were not needed, because in August 1914 patriotic feeling in Russia prevailed over popular discontent.

Chapter 5

Railways in the First World War

T he inescapable dependence of the continental powers on a
rapid railborne mobilization and concentration has led more
than one commentator to describe August 1914 as 'war by timetable'. The question of how far the railway mobilization plans
made war inevitable, once one country had ordered mobilization,
is an important line of enquiry in the search for the causes of the
First World War. Certainly the Germans, whose Schlieffen Plan
was absolutely dependent on a rapid mobilization and a quick
victory over France before the bulk of the Russian army reached
the front, could not afford to delay once the Russians began to
mobilize. Tsar Nicholas II and his government were quite aware
of this, and did try to delay general mobilization. A partial
Russian mobilization against Austria alone was announced, only
to be cancelled the next day because the army chief-of-staff had
realized that there was no mobilization plan which included
Austria but excluded Germany. So the Tsar signed the order of
general mobilization, only to revoke this order a few hours later,
well aware of what the decision meant. Then he was prevailed
upon the next day to change his mind again. He signed the
order once more and this time it did mean war.

Whether Russia's mobilization should have meant war is
another matter. Subsequent historians who support the 'war by
timetable' interpretation of the causes of the First World War,
point out that once mobilization started, it could not be stopped
without dislocating all the intricate railway transportation plans,
plans which had taken many staff officers months and sometimes

years of labour to work out. Thus a nation which halted its
mobilization and deployment in mid-air would inevitably disorganize its entire military posture, making it an easy victim if its
enemies should decide to go ahead with their own deployment.
Technically, however, there seems no reason why the powers
could not have halted their mobilization process for those few
vital days which, in some historians' opinion, would have sufficed
to solve the Serbian crisis diplomatically.

To take the worst possible case, a halt to the mobilization
process just as the great mass of troops (the 'third category' in the
German scheme) was being deployed to its battle stations at the
front would have been possible for all the belligerents. Armies in
trains are very easily handled, and there would have been little
difficulty in using the railway telegraph to stop all trains until
further notice. Such an order, especially if it were in force for

*A German rail-mounted heavy gun in action in 1917. The nickname applied
to such weapons, 'Big Bertha', was said to have been derived from Bertha
Krupp, whose company manufactured the guns*

more than a day, would certainly have raised acute problems. The first of these would have been the problem of finding food for the horses. The second, considerably less pressing, would have been the question of finding food for the men. But, after all, the mobilization took place at harvest time and—as the German offensive through France in August demonstrated—it was still possible for even the vast armies of 1914 to live off the land in the summer. From the railways' point of view the problem would have been to keep locomotives watered, fuelled and manned over an uncertain period. But this, even in Russia, was by no means insoluble, especially as the majority of trains would have been halted at railway yards, well provided with supplies and personnel.

The problem, therefore, was not so much the impossibility of stopping the trains, but the military staffs' conviction that it was impossible. Since mobilization plans were divided into Day 1, Day 2 and so on there was no organizational problem as long as the order in which the trains followed each other was not altered.

If trains were stopped on Day 5, they could be restarted on any day merely by calling that day Day 6. Admittedly though, a *reversal* of the plan would have been far more complex; if a diplomatic solution had been reached while the trains were halted it seems doubtful whether even the most resourceful railway managements could have immediately returned the troops back to their starting points.

The real, as opposed to the formal, beginning of the war can be taken as 2 August, when German troops first crossed the frontier. Before this, however, the German railways had already been busy with war traffic. On 28 July guards had been stationed at bridges along the main railways and those army units earmarked as cover for the deployment were returned from training camps to their permanent quarters. On the last day of July, following a government statement that war was imminent, guards were stationed along the key railway lines, rail traffic across the frontiers ceased, and civilian freight traffic was halted in the anticipated war areas (that is, west of the Rhine, south of the line Aachen to Cologne, and east of the line Bromberg–Poznan–Breslau–Neisse). Frontier defence troops were embarked, the military horsebreeding establishments of eastern Prussia evacuated, and rolling stock near the frontiers not considered essential for military use was brought back into the interior. Meanwhile civilian passenger traffic increased as Germans hurried home from their holidays and 65,000 Italian residents, unsure whether Italy would be an ally or enemy of Germany, bought tickets for the south. On 1 August, mobilization day, this civilian traffic was at its height with the Prussian State Railways alone providing 235 special trains. 2 August was Day No. 1 of the German mobilization. Freight traffic ceased, with freight cars taken to appointed stations to be unloaded and then allocated for military use. Many of them had their sides removed to make the flatcars needed for the transport of guns and artillery carts. New loading and unloading platforms were erected, and a few short branches laid.

The operation against Luxemburg, whose territory and railways were needed for the deployment of the German army, was a purely railway operation, planned well in advance. An armoured train was sent across the frontier shortly after midnight, followed by elements of an infantry division in their special trains. This captured Luxembourg and its entire railway network.

On 4 August the war timetables were introduced, and fast passenger trains were eliminated. However, ordinary passenger services continued and were used by reservists called up to their units. The main military movements, which had begun on 2 August, reached great intensity on 4, 5 and 6 August. Among the first troops to embark were six infantry brigades destined for the capture of Liège in Belgium, needed because of its status as a vital railway junction. Towards the evening of 6 August the strategic deployment began, with most troops being sent to the left bank of the Rhine. Some lines were used very intensively; the Hohenzollern Bridge over the Rhine near Cologne carried 2,150 westbound military trains between 2 and 18 August—one train every ten minutes.

Nevertheless, the German railways were never extended to their full capacity during this period; they could have carried even more traffic. Over three million military passenger-journeys were recorded, as well as the carriage of 860,000 horses and many thousands of tons of supplies. About 11,000 trains were required, and unexpected delays were few. The most serious 'incident' was when the commander of the 3rd Army demanded that two of his corps should be disembarked farther to the west than originally planned. This caused some confusion, affecting other trains, and finally the military railway service officials decided to take a strong line with the commander responsible. Evidently the Germans knew how to handle conflicts between military and transportation requirements.

With the other powers things went equally well. The Russian railways did so well that they found capacity to restore their freight trains to service, rather sheepishly reloading the freight that had been jettisoned at wayside stations a couple of weeks earlier. Formally, at least, the Russians handled the problem of railwaymen's liability to military service very well. Whereas the German railways were seriously embarrassed in the mobilization period by the loss of reservists called to the colours, in Russia reservists who worked on the railways were only technically called up, and in fact allowed to stay at their job. However, workers in railway workshops were not included in this dispensation, which caused widespread discontent and led to serious problems later.

In France, key operating workers were also spared call-up, but in fact thousands left their jobs to volunteer in the first few weeks,

again causing serious difficulties. But in general the French
railways did well. The General Staff's Plan No. XVII, drawn up
in 1913 and in force from April 1914, envisaged a traffic density
of 56/24 on the main strategic double-track routes. The plan
covered the first sixteen days after mobilization. In the first
eleven days the most urgently needed combatants were to be
carried, together with their supplies. Then there was to be a
twelve-hour break, in which the railways could catch up with
any delays, followed by the remaining five days. The military
commissars attached to the railways were warned on 26 July that
war was imminent, and on 30 July a few discreet preparations
were made. The *transports de couverture* (covering echelons) of
troops to defend the deployment areas were begun on 31 July
and finished on 3 August; these trains were additional to the
civilian timetables, which were maintained in this period. The
mobilization proper was effected with regular or special trains,
taking reservists from their home stations to the stations serving the
depots to which they reported. From these depots the units were
sent to their place in the deployment scheme by the *transports de
concentration* (concentration echelons). In all, it took twenty days
to complete mobilization and deployment. During this time
forty-two French army corps were deployed, each corps requiring
on average eighty trains of fifty vehicles. By 19 August France's
five armies were in their assigned positions; over one million men
and 400,000 horses had been successfully transported to the
frontiers. At Troyes, perhaps the most important junction of the
Est Railway, more than 400 trains were passed on some days,
implying a train every four minutes. This pressure meant that
accidents did happen. At the end of the first week there was a
series of mishaps near Troyes, blocking important lines for many
hours. But the military transport officers, by postponing one or
two trains and re-routing others, coped well with the situation.
There was no serious confusion and only a few trains were
affected; evidently the railway plans were more flexible than
their authors had dared to hope.

The French accidents were almost always the result of rear-end
collisions, and were wisely ascribed to fatigue on the part of the
railwaymen, who had already lived through a week of strenuous
and unsettling operation. For the ordinary railwayman, mobilization was an upsetting of his whole rhythm of work. Trains came
from unaccustomed directions and at unaccustomed times, they

were far more numerous, and congestion always seemed to be imminent. There were new officials and new fellow-workers. Familiar faces disappeared. There seemed to be no timetable. Locomotive crews had to travel over unfamiliar routes and although they were each accompanied by a local pilotman they were naturally ill at ease. And all the time the emphasis was on speed and regularity. In these conditions it is hardly surprising that there were accidents.

In France, railway demolition had begun during the deployment period. At the same time as locomotives were withdrawn from locomotive depots like that at Conflans, dangerously close to the frontier, a few bridges were also blown. After a few days it was clear that some of these early demolitions had been premature. In peacetime, selected structures, mainly bridges, had been provided with pockets for demolition charges, and the explosives were kept nearby. Preparation for demolition was assigned to joint teams of military and railway permanent way staff. The order for destruction could be given by officers and in certain cases officials. This broad category was one reason why some bridges were blown unnecessarily; nine local bridges were ordered to be destroyed by one prefect as 'a simple measure of strategic prudence'; a few days later sappers were studying their reconstruction. On the Est Railway 139 structures were equipped for demolition, and during the period of the German Schlieffen Plan, between 22 August and 9 September, twenty-seven were blown. In their subsequent retreat the Germans blew a further seventeen. On the Nord Railway the destruction was even greater. This railway, which adjoined Belgium, also had the problem of evacuating about one million refugees in the first few weeks. There was also the Belgian rolling stock which had been withdrawn into France, and had to be transported further into the interior. There were over 1,250 Belgian locomotives, which were laid up in dumps to await the anticipated reconquest of Belgium. When this failed to take place many units were taken over by the British and French. A batch was also sent by sea to help the Russian railways, only to be finally captured by the Germans in the Second World War.

(overleaf) *A locomotive tests the bridge built in 1918 over the Canal du Nord at Havrincourt, France, by a reserve company of German railway construction troops*

It was over the territory of the Nord Railway that the German offensive advanced and the rapidity of the attack made the withdrawal of rolling stock a delicately timed affair; if the cars and locomotives were withdrawn too soon, French supply trains would be affected, but if it was left too late, the Germans would acquire and use the material. The Nord, however, succeeded in withdrawing all but seventy-four of its locomotives, most of which were immobilized in workshops. At the peak of the German offensive, the Nord's mileage was reduced from 2,400 to just 940 miles and of this residue the two truncated main lines were connected only by a heavily graded single-track line.

The deployment of the British Expeditionary Force was one of the heaviest burdens for the French railways; in this case the Nord and Etat railways. Although before the war the 4th Bureau had prepared a plan, this could be little more than a rough forecast, for the arrival of the British units in France could be planned neither in terms of time nor of volume. The state of the weather and the availability of shipping were two other unknown elements. Moreover, the British mobilization was not expected to coincide precisely with that of the French; indeed, it was not certain that the British would go to war at all. However, it was established that the British would disembark at Le Havre, Rouen and Boulogne and would be deployed in the area between Busigny and the Belgian frontier. Two rail routes, both passing through Amiens, were allocated to this movement. The first British units arrived on 12 August, and were entrained the following day. Because each ship brought a different number of men, and because the units were themselves so varied in size, the railways found it impracticable to use standard train compositions, so several types of train were assembled, each distinguished by its own letter. These trains were mainly operated from Le Havre. In total there were 361, carrying 115,000 men and 46,000 horses.

The British troops arrived just in time to enter Belgium to meet the German forces, which had embarked upon the second stage of the Schlieffen Plan on 12 August; the first stage had been the occupation of Luxemburg and the capture of the Belgian railway junction at Liège. The need to pass through Belgium, which helped to ensure that Britain would enter the war, was itself a consequence of the railway situation. For in order to avail itself of the maximum number of railway connections with the interior of Germany, the German army had to occupy as wide-embracing an area as possible, which meant that its advance could only be on a wide front, wide enough to include Belgium. In all, five armies participated, from the First Army marching through Belgium to the Fifth Army passing through Luxemburg. The First Army had the longest distance to march, as it was on the outside of the planned wheeling movement against Paris. The French and Belgians were expected to put their railways out of action as they retreated and ninety companies of railway troops were to accompany the leading German units to put things right. These companies had their work trains prepared in advance with all the equipment they were expected to need for their task.

The Schlieffen Plan was weakest in its logistical aspects. Many awkward problems had not been solved, in the hope that when the day came unforeseen circumstances, luck and improvisation would solve all difficulties. While the army marched forward, the railway behind it would be restored so that railheads would never be so far behind the advance that horse transport could not bridge the gap. In the event, however, the German armies did advance much faster than their railheads, and horse transport could not cope with the distribution of supplies. While French demolition was just as thorough as had been expected, the hope that the Belgians would not destroy their own railways proved unfounded. Demolition of Belgian tunnels was especially disconcerting. And not only were structures demolished, but almost all serviceable locomotives were evacuated into France. Thus at times the German advance was seventy or eighty miles ahead of the railheads. The shortfall was made good by living off the land to an extent previously thought impossible. But fodder for the horses was a problem; sometimes they were fed green corn, which for many was fatal. The German army, just like the Russian at this period, had attached too much importance to cavalry. This arm, apart from being of little use in modern warfare, put a great strain on supply services; in Russia a cavalry division of 4,000 men needed as many trains as an infantry division of 16,000. In the railway age cavalry did not enhance an army's mobility, but reduced it.

Interestingly, the good management and exemplary co-ordination between railwaymen and officers which typified the interior German railways at this period was not in evidence when the German lines were extended into the newly conquered

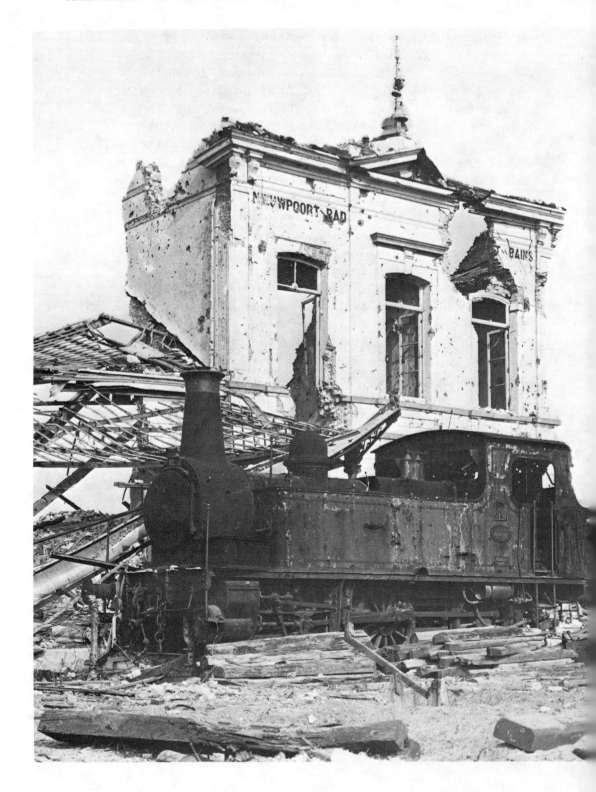

territory. Most of the lessons which were supposed to have been taught by the American Civil War had to be learned again by some German officers. The destruction of delicate signalling apparatus meant that the newly restored lines could not pass many trains in safety, but nevertheless the military authorities insisted on pushing through the greatest possible number of trains, with the result that congestion developed, especially as there was little chance to send back empty cars. Local commanders, putting the supply of their own men before all else, unloaded for their own benefit trains destined for other units and commandeered freight cars for use as magazines or storehouses. Some trains never reached their intended unit because those units had been diverted elsewhere without notification to the transport authority. Meanwhile the odd freight car, loaded with gifts for the boys from the women back home, floated around the railway network because no commander was going to waste time unloading them.

As the five German armies marched on their broad front from the east and north, the French railway officers had to improvise plans for moving reinforcements from the south-east. Although these plans were worked out and executed at the most difficult time—during a fast retreat when detraining points could be overrun by the enemy even as the trains of reinforcements were still on the move—they were carried out by the French railways with great flexibility. Because the Paris–Nancy main line was expected to be cut by the advancing Germans, many trains took a roundabout route over the Paris–Lyons–Méditerranée Railway. It is true that the 21st Corps arrived half a day late to counter a fierce German attempt to make a penetration, but the Corps, embarked in sixty-four trains from 4 to 6 September, had actually been despatched to another destination and was switched to the critical area while in passage.

Another corps, the 15th, was transported by rail for just fifty kilometres in order to arrive at the battlefield sooner and fresher. To carry troops such a short distance was normally regarded as inefficient, but the results were worthwhile on this occasion. A. Marchand, who was the military transport officer arranging

Contrary to German expectations, nearly all Belgian locomotives were evacuated to France. Here, one of the few that were left behind stands in the wrecked station of Niewpoort in 1917

this movement, later wrote about it in his book *Les Chemins de Fer de l'Est et la Guerre*:

'Commandant Marchand then went to the army head-quarters at Ligny. There was a rapid conversation with the chief of staff . . .

"What can you do?"

"Whatever you want, so long as there are only infantry units to transport."

"Agreed. When?"

"When you wish."

"How far can you send the trains?"

"As far as you wish."

"That's perfect."

'The details were quickly fixed. The two columns of the 15th Corps consisted of the southern column which, in advance of the other, would reach Gondrecourt at the end of the day, and the northern, which would arrive only during the night. The first would therefore be loaded as soon as it appeared, and the second from 01.00 the next morning. The latter would embark at Mauvages so as to avoid a night march to Gondrecourt. The infantrymen would be embarked at the rate of one and a half battalions per train, and their horses and wagons would be carried in two supplementary trains. . . . The trains would follow one another at the rate of three each hour. The infantry would embark on the platforms of Gondrecourt station itself, while the horses and carts would be loaded into the trains at the military platform. . . . The troops arrive towards 16.00. Understanding is soon reached with the unit commanders. Two trains are loaded at a time. The first leaves at 17.00 and the last at 20.20. Disembarkation is as requested by the army, at Longeville and Nanois . . . in the morning of the 8 a brigade is sent west to Robert-Espagne, outflanking an attack by the German XVIII reserve corps. The other brigade, held in reserve at first near Contrisson, then attacks to the north, joined by the 2nd division of 15th Corps which has arrived after embarking in trains early on the 8 at Mauvages in the same way as the 1st Division had embarked at Gondrecourt.

'The transport had required 19 trains. It is an apt example of the application of railway transport at the right time during a battle, providing immediate action. On 9 September the German retreat started. . . .'

In general, Marchand added, to move a corps during operations required on average eighteen hours to make arrangements and collect rolling stock and a total time of from three to four days. This presupposed a traffic intensity of 36/24, and five or six embarkation points.

Marchand's troop movements were part of the Battle of the Marne, which signalled the failure of the Schlieffen Plan. When the French armies stood before Paris they were faced by German armies which were not only worn out by their long march and weakened by lack of supplies, but also very much reduced in numbers by the need to leave soldiers behind to guard the supply railways against possible *francs-tireurs*. In a few days the pursued became the pursuers as the Germans retreated to protect their threatened flanks. It was now the turn of the French to restore railways already damaged once by themselves and then again by the Germans. Thanks partly to this demolition, the Germans extricated themselves without any great disaster. Meanwhile on the Eastern Front, on a smaller scale but over longer distances, railways had played a similar role. In East Prussia the Russians were able to mount an offensive sooner than either they or the Germans had expected, but after early success they were defeated at Tannenberg. For this battle the Germans were able to deploy troops from the Western Front by means of their railways.

Thus, at this peculiar stage of military transport history, when the railway systems were highly developed but motor transport still insufficient, it was evident that defenders had a great advantage. Their own supply railways were intact, while the attacking enemy had to cope with unfamiliar and damaged railway routes. The Schlieffen Plan was the nearest the Germans could come to a Blitzkrieg in the First World War; speed of advance was still held back by dependence on the horse-drawn cart plying between railhead and front-line unit, although speedier track-laying and the use of military light railways went some way to reducing this dependence.

Each of the powers had its own railway organization, and its own way of dividing authority between railwaymen and the military. In Germany, as already mentioned, the entire railway network fell under military control. A given corps had its originating station in the interior, from which supplies could be shipped down a nominated main line to the war zone. The war zone was divided into two belts. In the staging area the supplies were reassembled for sending forward to units as re-supply kits, and were unloaded in the second operational belt, the military area just behind the front line. From here they were taken to units by road or by narrow-gauge railway.

In France the railways were divided into two networks, those of the interior zone, which were operated and controlled by railwaymen, and those of the military zone, which were under military control. The military zone was divided into the rear zone, which could be 100 miles wide, and the narrower advanced zone. A feature of the French system were the regulating stations, situated in the rear zone. These were key junctions, provided with offices for the military controllers, extensive sidings, warehouses, unloading platforms, switching yards, depots for artillery, engineer, supply, and health services, a base for railway troops and their repair trains, and facilities for hospital trains. Originally it had been hoped that each army would be served by one regulating station, but in practice this was impossible. In peacetime Rheims was regarded as the ideal regulating station, and officers graduating from the Ecole Supérieure de Guerre who expected to join the 4th Bureau visited that station to familiarize themselves with its possibilities.

In the deployment period, troop trains passed through the regulating station without break of bulk. At the time of despatch from the corps' originating station in the rear the trains were issued with orders specifying only their regulating station; the final destination was not given. On arrival at the regulating station the military transport commission completed the train documents by filling in the disembarkation point. The train was then sent forward, but with a spare locomotive crew and a carload of extra coal in case of any unforeseen delays. The locomotive men were also given a document allowing them to work over lines which were unfamiliar to them. After the deployment period, the system changed. Supply trains in one direction and evacuation trains in the other were unloaded, or at least reassembled, at the regulating stations. Supplies were assembled in trains, or groups of freight cars, destined for individual units. To supply a corps, a regulating station was at first expected to need each day fifty cars for 100,000 men, but this figure had grown to 150 cars by 1918. From its warehouses, and from loaded cars waiting in their respective sidings, thirty-car trains were assembled. In 1914 such a train included eight carloads of bread, two of miscellaneous foodstuffs, twelve of oats, one car for the corps' mail, and another for its baggage; four cars for personnel and for evacuating sick and wounded, and two standard luggage vans. Units were expected to find their own meat and hay supplies. At the front-line supply station the train was unloaded and its contents sent forward by road or narrow-gauge railway.

It was accepted that neither narrow-gauge railways nor motor transport could replace the standard-gauge railway as the main artery of supply. In 1916, the celebrated column of motor trucks which supplied besieged Verdun along the '*Voie Sacrée*' was really nothing more than an improvisation which should not have been necessary. The military authorities had neglected to provide Verdun with an alternative railway when the existing line came within range of German shellfire. They further hampered the city's defence by transferring responsibility for railway transport in the area from one regulating station to another, which, though nearer, had no experience in that sector. In the end, rather late in the day, a new sixty-kilometre supply railway was laid. Until this was built to supplement the motor trucks the only line available was a pre-war metre-gauge light railway. This, the Meusienne Railway, was especially vital in the early weeks of the German attack, and seventy-five locomotives were drafted to it from other French metre-gauge lines, as well as some 800 cars. There were all kinds of complications because the drafted equipment had different couplings, different brakes and different basic dimensions; but somehow the trains were formed and despatched. Sometimes as many as thirty-four daily trains were operated, and after particularly bloody battles this little line took out more than 600 wounded in a day.

In offensive actions the railway's role was to bring forward the means of attack, and to stand ready to exploit success by extending its services into the conquered territory. The high commands soon realized that this meant that it was no longer practicable to seek the surprise element. An extending network of narrow-gauge lines, new dumps and increased railway activity were sure signs to the enemy that an offensive was being prepared. Geographical surprise was henceforth out of the question, because the preparations for weeks previously were virtually inscribed on the terrain; surprise of timing, however, was still possible to some extent. After a break-through, railway troops were sent to restore railways damaged by the retreating enemy. The high commands chose

their points of attack with the railway situation in mind. Not only
did they try to launch their offensives in places where their own
troops were well supplied with standard-gauge lines, but they
aimed their attacks at areas where the enemy's railway communications were weak or, better still, could easily be cut at an
early stage of the advance.

The 1915 French Champagne campaign offers a good example
of the role of railways in offensive operations. This offensive (see
map below) was to be launched northwards from a zone between
two south–north railway lines, one from St Hilaire-au-Temple to

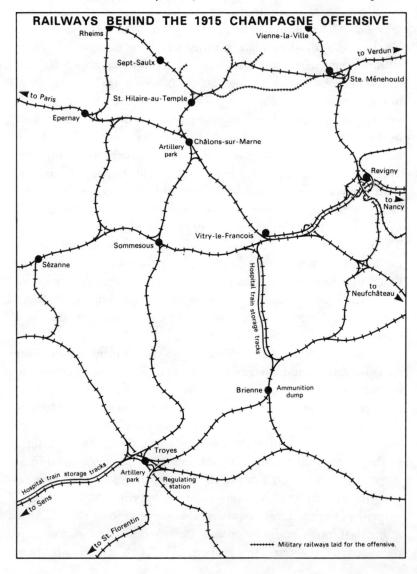

RAILWAYS BEHIND THE 1915 CHAMPAGNE OFFENSIVE

Rheims
Vienne-la-Ville
to Verdun ▶
Sept-Saulx
Ste. Ménehould
◀ to Paris
St. Hilaire-au-Temple
Epernay
Châlons-sur-Marne
Artillery park
Revigny
to ▶ Nancy
Vitry-le-Francois
Sommesous
Hospital train storage tracks
Sézanne
to Neufchâteau ▶
Brienne
Ammunition dump
Troyes
Hospital train storage tracks
Artillery park
Regulating station
◀ to Sens
to St. Florentin
••••••• Military railways laid for the offensive.

Sept-Saulx and the other from Ste Ménehould to Vienne-la-Ville. The continuations southwards of these two lines, to the junctions at Troyes and Vitry-le-François respectively, were to be the main supply lines of the attack. There were in addition two lines parallel to the front. One of these, from Châlons to Revigny via Vitry-le-François, was part of the Paris–Nancy main line and very well equipped. Between Vitry and Revigny it was paralleled by another west–east line, which meant that there were four tracks available between those two points. Farther north, close to the line, was the key line from St Hilaire to Ste Ménehould. This had been prepared for intense traffic by the introduction of block signalling, but it was only single track, and was within range of the German guns. A new line was therefore built parallel to it by railway troops. This was also single track, but was out of shellfire range. It was provided with several transhipment stations, including some single-platform stations of 400 metres, where standard-gauge trains could stop on one side to tranship their freight to narrow-gauge trains on the other. The 60 cm gauge network of field railways was considerably augmented, with the aim of assembling as much material as close as possible to the front. Meanwhile, from July (when the planning stage began) to the end of September (when the attack was launched), other improvements were made. Notable among these was the re-signalling of the south–north supply line between Revigny and Ste Ménehould. By increasing the number of block sections the capacity of this line was raised to six trains per hour. Farther back, storage tracks were laid for heavy artillery trains and for hospital trains, which were expected to move up to the front quite soon after the start of the battle. For the preliminary bombardment, a number of rail-mounted guns were placed on specially built firing tracks laid from railways close to the front.

The attack was launched on 25 September on a fifteen-mile front. Some units advanced two miles on the first day, but the Germans were able to bring up reinforcements and little further progress was made; by mid-October the offensive had plainly failed to make a breakthrough. Nevertheless, the railways had done their duty faultlessly and the same techniques would be used in future offensive operations. Under the control of the Troyes regulating station over 3,000 trains had been operated, the two south to north lines each carrying over sixty pairs of trains on some crucial days.

The most outstanding offensive of the war was that undertaken by the Russian General Brusilov against Austria in 1916. It was remarkable in that it was undertaken with inferior railway support. In his memoirs Brusilov commented: 'Knowing the limitations of our rail transport . . . I knew that while we were entraining and transporting one Army Corps, the Germans would manage to transport three or four.' He therefore asked that troops should not be sent to him from other regions since they would reveal his intentions to the enemy and moreover arrive after the enemy's own reinforcements. Having more or less abandoned the idea of a great concentration of troops, Brusilov did manage to surprise the Austrians with his attack, which made a spectacular breakthrough. Inevitably, however, supply difficulties soon brought it to a halt.

Of the great railway powers, the Russians were the least successful in co-ordinating the work of railwaymen with military requirements. As in France, the railway network was divided into two regions. The ministry of transport and its railway managers continued to operate the railways of the interior, while an ever-widening belt in the west came under military control. About one-third of the total mileage was thereby militarized, and at one stage even the capital, Petrograd, was included in the war zone. The western railways were thus split between civilian and military control, but whereas in France this situation had been acceptable, the lack of co-operation between professionals and soldiers made it virtually unworkable in Russia. While the railwaymen were slow to change their routines for the sake of urgent military requirements, the army officers refused to co-operate by adapting their needs to the legitimate requirements of successful railway operation. In particular, local commanders accumulated empty railway cars. Among other industries, the Donets coal basin was handicapped because empty coal cars had to be returned via railways passing through the military zone, and army commanders commandeered them for their own use as warehouses, offices, living quarters and 'in case of need'. Only in January 1917 were all the railways brought under the control of the transport ministry, but by then it was too late. Transport failure, partly due to a backlog of locomotives awaiting repair, but in large part due to the shortage of empty cars, led to food shortages in the cities and so to internal unrest; it was a bread shortage in Petrograd which triggered the Russian Revolution.

When the Revolution occurred, the Russian railways were just about to receive 875 2-10-0 locomotives built in the USA and Canada. These had been ordered because domestic suppliers had long been operating a cartel and were not willing to build locomotives at the price which the government offered. The Revolution meant that not all of these were delivered, and some were sold to US railroads. In the Second World War, however, a further batch was built, and these were delivered to the Soviet government. But while locomotive-building stagnated in wartime Russia, new lines were built rapidly, usually to shorten hard-pressed routes. At the time of the Revolution there were about 13,330 kilometres of line under construction.

The February Revolution in Russia was followed by mass desertions from the army as peasant soldiers rushed to regain their villages in anticipation of a share-out of land. In their passage they took the first trains they could find, often wrecking the interiors of passenger cars in their riotous exuberance. The sudden release from military discipline was too much for the war-weary soldiers, especially when they were travelling in groups. Passenger class distinctions were ignored, car interior fittings purloined or broken, and ordinary passengers insulted, beaten up, robbed or ejected from the trains.

The French railways were already familiar with this problem, on a less intense scale. In the summer of 1915 the French command decided that, since the front had become static, leave could be granted to the troops. Little preparation was made for this decision and the transport arrangements were therefore somewhat improvised. It was agreed that soldiers would leave their units either by ordinary train or by supply trains returning empty from the front. On arrival at the regulating station they would be sent on to the military assembly station of their home region, and then they would take an ordinary train to their home station. But while this scheme seemed theoretically sound, it proved different in practice. All too often a *permissionnaire*, having received his leave pass and his travel documents, discovered that there was neither convenient supply train nor ordinary train, and no soldier wants to spend the first day of his leave waiting for a train. There could be other delays at the regulating station and at the assembly station, neither of which was intended to handle large flows of *permissionnaires*. Extra services had to be operated, but even these were not popular because their schedules did not seem to give the soldier the maximum possible time at home. In particular, men returning from leave preferred to take the civilian passenger trains. These were already overcrowded, so that returning *permissionnaires* often took them virtually by assault. Front-line men, released from the imminence of death for a few days, and from the iron discipline of the front, were in a mood only to enjoy themselves, and to be treated with the deference traditionally granted to the condemned. Discipline broke down. Trains were damaged and civilian passengers molested. By early 1918 the railways operated about 3,500 special leave trains each month, and despite the regulations, despite General Pétain's *Guide du permissionnaire*, thousands of soldiers still preferred to break the rules and travel on civilian trains. Railway transport officers were instructed to take things in hand, but to have done so would have meant neglecting their other duties. Special train-changing stations for *permissionnaires* were set up; these served on the one hand as termini for trains to and from the front, and on the other, for special trains running to the major population centres. Such a station would pass about 120,000 *permissionnaires* per month on the homeward trip, and perhaps 100,000 on the return flow. This discrepancy was simply a result of the large number of soldiers refusing to take the leave trains for the return trip. Apart from those who found the civilian services more convenient there were many whose reluctance to return to the trenches led them to cruise up and down the railways, pretending to be lost. At the exchange stations amenities were provided in an attempt to attract the wanderers; canteens, cinematograph halls, toilets, transport advice offices were all set up. But by the end of the war the problem was still far from a solution.

The extra burden of *permissionnaires* on the civilian services would have been less serious if the French railways by 1917 had not been so run down. In general, the railways performed well during the war, but there was a so-called transport crisis in the winter of 1916–17. The basic cause of this was that whereas during the war traffic had increased by about fifty per cent, the number of available locomotives and cars had actually diminished. France began the war with 13,800 locomotives, of which only 6,000 had been built since 1898. Deliveries from domestic works were minimal during the war, and the number of locomotives awaiting repair doubled. The transfer of locomotives to the more hard-pressed railways was one reason for the delay in returning

THE LEAVE STATION AT FAVRESSE

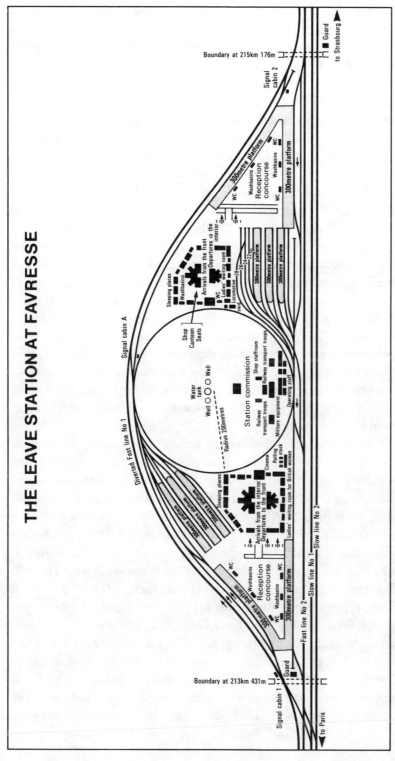

Source: Marchand, Les Chemins de Fer de l'Est et la Guerre

unserviceable locomotives to traffic because, unlike Russia and Germany, France did not have a standard freight locomotive that could be moved from railway to railway without creating a spare parts problem. G. Lafon, in his *Les Chemins de Fer Français pendant la guerre*, gave one perhaps extreme comment about this: '. . . we have seen vehicles needing a one-hour repair put on one side . . . for two years because of lack of spares. When the spares at last arrived from the owning railway the vehicles were irreparable due to deterioration from the weather.' However, the difficulties were blamed on the priority given to military traffic over civilian, which, it was said, was acceptable for a short war but not for three years. So a succession of measures was taken, which resulted in the Ministry of Public Works, not the military authorities, having control over the railways of both zones. However, the Minister was assisted by a general as his Director-General of Military Transport and this general in fact played the role of chief executive officer. In this way, it was claimed, ultimate civilian authority was provided at the same time as the military, in practice, continued to organize their own transport. Other measures to ease the strain on the railways were the introduction of normal work on Sundays, the exclusion from fast trains of low-priority freight, a three-category priority system for freight and, in April 1917, general permission to load freight cars beyond their nominal capacity.

Rather belatedly, the French railway companies did meet to discuss the standardization of equipment, but little was decided which could be of immediate benefit. Orders for locomotives and rolling stock were placed in Britain and America. The engines built in Britain were 2-8-0s of French design, a few of which were among the last steam locomotives to work on French railways. Also in 1916 the French government asked the British to take over the task of supplying the British Expeditionary Force in France; hitherto it had been the French, mainly the Nord Railway, who were responsible for this considerable traffic.

The British Army's Railway Operating Division (ROD) had begun work in France in 1915, but before then there had been railway troops active overseas. In 1914 the South Eastern & Chatham Railway extended its operations to Boulogne, where it sent ten yard locomotives and various employees to help with the dockyards. At about the same time construction companies, largely recruited from British railways' platelayers, were sent to north-eastern France to repair and maintain the standard- and metre-gauge lines that supplied the British Expeditionary Force. Additional construction companies were organized throughout the war, and in France alone laid hundreds of miles of new line as well as repairing damaged sections. To help supply the necessary rail, the British railways in 1917 closed enough of their branch lines to enable 200 miles of track to be sent to France. At the close of the war British and Canadian railway troops helped to restore the Belgian railways; the last of their 'temporary' bridges survived until 1930.

The first line operated by the ROD—a section of the Haze-brouck–Ypres line—was entrusted to a company of former London & North Western Railway employees in mid-1916. By the end of the war about 800 miles of track were being operated in France by this service, as well as about 1,000 miles of light railways. By that time, too, the number of British railway troops in France totalled almost 75,000, although not all these were former railwaymen; men found unsuitable for front-line service were often sent as labourers to the railway units. In general, the ROD became responsible for moving troops and supplies over the long haul from the ports to the regulating stations; between the latter and the British front, the French retained responsibility. However, because on some sections of line the British contingent of locomotives and drivers working alongside the French was quite considerable, it became quite common for the British to handle French civilian traffic—passenger as well as freight. In the early days of the ROD, evacuated Belgian locomotives were the main-stay of operations, but British engines arrived in increasing numbers during the final two years of the war, as the French, quite naturally, had no intention of relinquishing the 600-odd locomotives that they had been using for the British trains.

The first British locomotives to arrive were contributed by twelve railway companies. Totalling about 600 units, they were mainly of the 0-6-0 type and sometimes of great age. Only the Great Central's nineteen 0-6-0s could be described as modern representatives of their type, together with eleven Great Western Railway 2-6-0s so new that they had never run in ordinary service. The Great Western also contributed eighty-four

(overleaf) *On the British-operated railways in northern France: a standard (Great Central) locomotive lies on its side after a mishap, as a supply train passes over the repaired line*

middle-aged six-wheelers. These locomotives were later supplemented by over 300 units of the Ministry of Munitions standard 2-8-0, which was a copy of a standard Great Central Railway freight design, fitted with train heating equipment for working winter passenger trains, and with the continental steam brake. Most of these locomotives were transported to France on the army's train ferries, which in the final year of the war plied from a new port at Richborough to Calais and Dunkirk. The R O D also received 500 locomotives bought in America; these included 150 2-8-0 units built by Baldwin. In addition there were the hired locomotives from Belgium, and 'requisitioned' engines. The latter included ten freight engines, which had originally been built for the Trans-Australian Railway but which ended their days in Belgium, and, later, various German locomotives taken over at the Armistice.

France was not the only scene of activity for the British railway troops. The Salonika front and the Middle East were notable users of British rolling stock and railway troops. A great mileage of new railway, using metre-gauge track lifted from Indian branch lines, was laid in Mesopotamia; much of this still exists as part of the two-gauge Iraqi State Railways. Then there was the 260-mile line across the Sinai Desert and up to Haifa, the northern section of which is now part of Israeli Railways. A notable feature of the railway war in this region was the speed with which the British laid their lines, urgently needed as an essential part of the campaign plans. Also notable was the use by both British and Turks of aerial bombing against railway targets; because of the importance of the railways in these campaigns, the bombing effort directed against them was perhaps unequalled elsewhere in the war. In fact, the bombing had little permanent effect; railway lines were not easy to damage with the small bombs of that time. More damaging were the raids of Lawrence of Arabia and his men. The southern part of the Hedjaz Railway was put out of action for decades by Lawrence's attacks, although the reluctance to bring the line back into service suggests that it was not a particularly essential line of communication.

The arrival of American troops in 1918 placed an enormous burden on the French railways, leading to a minor transport crisis. Because of the all-out German offensives in the spring and summer of 1918, American troops landed in France in greater numbers than had been anticipated; over two million Americans were serving in France by the end of the war. As a result of this acceleration, ships that had been intended to carry transportation equipment were often used instead for moving troops and munitions. It had originally been intended that the US Transportation Corps would be sufficiently strong in men and equipment to handle all the American traffic, but this was never achieved. Because the Channel ports were overloaded, most Americans arrived through the Atlantic ports, notably Bordeaux and St Nazaire. They were transported by stages to the front along lines which had never been expected to carry such a heavy volume of traffic. In early 1918, therefore, considerable improvements had to be made to these new military routes, especially the lines from St Nazaire and Bordeaux to Bourges, and the line from Bourges to the American sector of the front. Such improvements included the lengthening of sidings to enable them to take the long American trains, the installation of block signalling and

Railways were a priority target in the Middle East campaigns. This picture shows a German-built locomotive of the Baghdad Railway put out of action at Samarrah. Running locomotives into turntable pits would be a favoured technique of saboteurs in the Second World War

the construction of chord lines where otherwise trains would have to reverse in order to pass from one line to another. New locomotive depots were built, and some new freight stations. The American infrastructure of warehouses, dumps, hospitals, leave centres and bases was served by newly laid sidings. Most of these works were carried out by the French, although one or two large undertakings were executed by the Transportation Corps.

At best, four-fifths of American traffic moved in American trains. The locomotives, mainly 2-8-0 'Pershing' units, were unloaded and reassembled at St Nazaire. The freight cars, which were of American type, had a thirty-ton capacity and were sent directly back to the ports when empty. Only a few lines were operated exclusively by Americans; in most cases American trains moved among French trains, and American personnel worked alongside French, with American movements being fitted into the French traffic pattern by a special regulating commission at Tours. For most of 1918 the American shipments moved smoothly, but there was a period of congestion in July when trains followed one another so closely that each crawled from one signal to the next. Sorting yards and junctions were so overworked that trains were delayed for hours. Train crews worked for eighteen hours or more at a time, and there was a spate of collisions and derailments. Meanwhile, while the complete trainloads were handled by American transportation troops, the single-carload shipments for the most part were despatched in French trains; this added to the pressure on the French system, especially as the distances from the western ports were above average.

The US Transportation Corps had 50,000 men in France by the end of the war. Most of these were former US railwaymen, and their training, as well as the training of those without any railway background, was completed after arrival in France, with French participation in the final stages. When this training was complete, the American operating staff were issued with documents allowing them to work on the French railways. The basic unit of the Corps was the battalion, of 750 men. Of these, 130 were attached to the battalion staff or did administrative work. Another 140 were labourers and clerks, and 480 were operating staff. One operating battalion was reckoned to be capable of managing a railway section of sixty miles, passing fifteen pairs of trains daily. There were also workshop and track battalions.

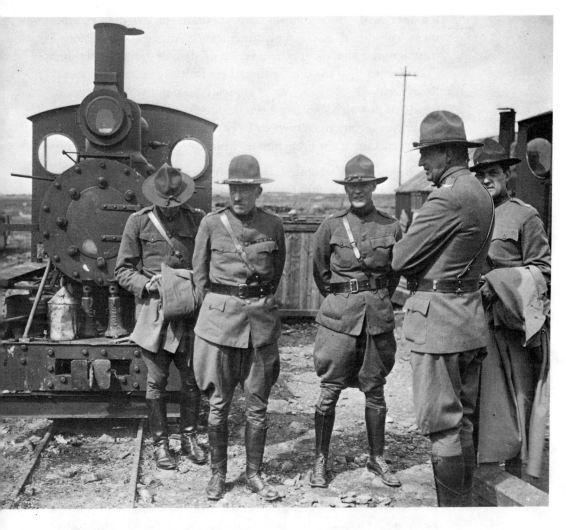

On the American light railways in France: General John Biddle, commanding the US railway regiments, visits the railway workshops at Boisleux au Mont in 1917

The earliest units to arrive seem to have been the best; the 13th Regiment, for example, won great admiration from the French for its smart operation of lines in the Meuse and Verdun area. Later arrivals were of poorer quality. At first the French shrugged their shoulders over the deficiencies of these later units, accepting that the best US railwaymen could not be recruited as they were needed at home. But after the Armistice there was some discord, at least on the Est Railway. The Americans stayed in France until mid-1919 and the post-war relaxation of discipline,

together with the unsatisfactory standard of original recruit-
ment, produced some ugly incidents. American locomotive
men ignored signals. Train crews halted their trains at stations
in order to go to the buffet. Est Railway pilotmen sometimes refused to ride on American locomotives because of
incidents in which they had been insulted while trying to persuade
American locomotive crews to work according to French operating rules. One irate Frenchman (Marchand) wrote:

> 'On the lines operated by the Americans there were daily
> robberies and vandalism. In certain stations, Longuyon for
> example, there were even armed attacks and there were many
> nights when fusillades could be heard. The American police
> intervened energetically, but they could not be everywhere. . . .
> American soldiers took passenger trains by assault and usually
> travelled without tickets and always in first class. . . .'

In November 1918, the American demobilization began. By
1 July, 1919, nearly two million troops had been transported back
to the ports. Since there were very few supply trains, the Transportation Corps was able to cope almost unaided with the task.
In the busiest month, May 1919, twelve demobilization trains
were run each day, with an average journey of 370 miles. After
the Americans had gone, however, almost all of the new railway
works built to handle this traffic were progressively abandoned;
the lines over which the Americans had moved were used very
little for French civilian or commercial traffic, so it was not worth
maintaining them. Here and there a new line or new signalling,
or even a new station or warehouse, was retained, and one line
kept the American 'despatcher' system of train control. Most of
the American locomotives stayed too, having been sold at
bargain prices by the American government. Many of them
survived to serve the US Army again after D-Day in 1944.

On the German side of the lines the transport situation was
different only in detail. On the whole the German railway supply
service coped with the situation as well as the French. It was only
in the final weeks of the war, when the German armies were in
retreat and desertion rates were high, that confusion and chaos
threatened to overwhelm the railways. Neither deserters nor
retreating units were in the mood to treat the railways with the
respect that they had hitherto enjoyed; individuals and fighting
units took over whatever railway facilities they could find without

any reference to the general situation or to railway operating requirements.

The German railway troops, after their initial difficulties during the first weeks of the war, did well, both in operating and in restoring lines. The failures of summer 1914 were in any case not qualitative; it was simply that the high command had not foreseen the scale of railway destruction that would be wreaked by the retreating French and Belgians. The railway repair battalions were not strong enough to repair this damage sufficiently fast to enable supply trains to follow closely after the German advance. German civilian engineering firms were finally brought in to help, but by then the Battle of the Marne was under way.

The railway troops were especially successful on the Eastern Front. Apart from supplying the German armies and transporting reinforcements faster than the Russians could move their own men, they quickly restored key railway lines in immense areas of newly occupied territory. Not only did they have to repair damage inflicted by the retreating Russians, they also had to cope with the gauge difference. Although there were cases of the Russian 5 ft gauge being maintained, with new lines of the same gauge built to connect with bases inside the German frontier, usually the Russian lines were re-gauged. By May 1916 the Germans had converted 4,700 miles to standard gauge, in Poland, White Russia and Lithuania. Because it was a case of narrowing rather than widening, the procedure was fairly simple: there were no clearance problems. It was sufficient to shift one rail 9 cm inwards. One railway troop detachment of two non-commissioned officers and thirty to thirty-four men was reckoned to be capable of re-gauging 1,100 to 1,500 yards per day. In bad weather progress was slower; snow, and especially melted snow which had re-frozen, was the worst hindrance. The usual Russian demolition procedure was to place a charge beneath every second rail joint. This damaged one end of each rail. The Germans coped with this by cutting off each damaged part, thereby accumulating a stock of shortened rails, which were then used for re-gauging. Towards the end of the war, however, the Russians introduced a heavy hook to tear cross-ties from the rails; this was hauled by the last locomotive to leave in the retreat and distorted most of the rails.

On both the Eastern and Western fronts, the Germans were

exceptionally well prepared for the use of narrow-gauge railways. Based on their experience in South West Africa, they had evolved their *Feldbahn* concept, which included a high standardization of equipment. They had, for example, a standard eight-wheeled locomotive design of which about 2,500 units were built by the end of the war. This was an exceptionally good machine; although it had eight coupled wheels it could cope with short-radius curves by virtue of an arrangement which enabled the leading and trailing pairs of coupled wheels to swivel and move sideways. However, horse power was also used on these 60 cm (2 ft) gauge lines, as on similar lines of the other belligerents. Since every infantry unit had its complement of horses, this form of traction was easily obtainable, and also easier to evacuate. It was on lines expected to be permanent, and with heavy traffic, that locomotives were used. Not all of these were steam; petrol tractors

The German version of the Décauville railway: troops move forward on the Feldbahn *laid near Menin in France, hauled by a petrol locomotive and travelling in vehicles quite luxurious in comparison with the French and British equivalents*

were especially valuable because they did not reveal their position by sparks and smoke. Steam lines in exposed positions were often limited to night operations because of their smoke problem, and even then it was common to fit tall spark-arresters on their chimneys.

The French, who regarded themselves as the inventors of the 60 cm gauge field railway, were also well prepared. Their standard locomotive was still the Pechot double-bogie, double-boiler eight-wheeler, but when the French began to introduce artillery railways they found themselves short of locomotive power. A hundred saddle-tank locomotives were ordered from Baldwin in the USA, later supplemented by some home-built 60 hp petrol rail-tractors. Before the war the French had already introduced petrol-electric rail-tractors on lines serving their frontier fortresses.

At the start of the war the Russians had nine railway battalions, of which three were narrow gauge. In addition, there were three brigades specializing in horse-traction lines. Five hundred and sixty miles of narrow-gauge field railways were already in operation, of which two-thirds were horse-operated. During the war an additional 1,300 miles of horse, 1,090 miles of steam and 140 miles of petrol narrow-gauge lines were laid. The Russians had perhaps the greatest need of such lines, given their undeveloped road system and their exceptionally long front line, fighting both the Germans and the Austrians. The Austrians, too, had a well-developed field railway service, their first narrow-gauge railway unit having been formed in 1873. Anticipating war in the Dolomites, the Austrians had realized that it would be hard to build standard-gauge lines on the Italian–Austrian front, so a proportionately heavier task had been allocated to the narrow-gauge lines, which were expected to be quite long. Indeed, in the long and usually fairly static campaign against Italy from 1915 to 1917 three substantial narrow-gauge lines were built by the Austrian Army; the line built by the Austrians from Auer to Predazzo, for instance, was thirty miles long, and included six tunnels and fourteen big bridges. These three lines were of 75 cm (2 ft 6 in) gauge, partly because of the extra capacity which that gauge provided and partly because there were already Italian-built 75 cm gauge lines in the vicinity. Special 2-6-6-0 Mallet-type tank locomotives were used on the Predazzo line until after the war, when the Italians converted it to metre gauge and electrified it for civilian use.

The British were late starters in this technique. The Boer War had suggested that twentieth-century warfare would be fast moving, in which case there would be little scope for field railways. A few so-called 'trench tramways' were envisaged, but that was all. After some months of static trench warfare in northern France, however, this opinion was modified and a network of 2 ft gauge lines was undertaken. This gauge was chosen in order to be compatible with the French system, although 2 ft 6 in would really have been preferred by the British, who had experience of that gauge in many parts of the Empire. Although a very capable 4-6-0 tank locomotive was built in Leeds for these lines, production was far from sufficient and orders were placed in the USA. The Baldwin Works produced 495 4-6-0 saddle tanks, which were strong, although somewhat top-heavy and rough-riding. Later the American Locomotive Company built a better design, a 2-6-2 side tank, for the British. Meanwhile the Baldwin Works, realizing the faults of their 4-6-0T, redesigned it as a 2-6-2, and built several hundreds for the use of the US Army in France.

All the belligerents, even the Germans, made greater use of narrow-gauge field railways than they had expected. Partly this was because of the static character of the war, but partly because these railways had an increasing range of uses. Before the war it had been generally recognized that they would be useful in serving advanced artillery emplacements; by bringing up ammunition they eliminated the perilous storage of munition stocks near the guns. Similarly they were ideal lines of communications for advanced fortifications; though as the traditional fortress was already regarded as obsolete in 1914, this field of activity seemed to have an unpromising future. But as the war progressed these lines proved invaluable, especially when roads had been destroyed by bombardment, by overuse, or by the weather. With freight cars of around ten tons capacity, the 2 ft gauge lines could carry most loads, although not in the quantities needed for a major offensive. In winter, and especially in muddy conditions, they were also appreciated as troop-carriers between the forward trenches and the rest areas. Other essential tasks which they performed included the evacuation of casualties and the supply of fresh water; ambulance cars carrying six stretcher cases and water tank cars were among the specialized types of rolling stock soon supplied to these lines. The steam locomotives themselves often ran short of water and it became the practice to equip them with 'water lifters', which enabled them to drop a flexible pipe into flooded shell holes and draw out the contents. Operations were usually very informal, even though the Germans and Austrians attempted to operate their lines according to standard railway practices. Derailments were frequent, and some locomotives were fitted with strong transverse metal beams just above the rails at each end; these were intended to act as bumpers to keep the locomotive on a comparatively even keel.

Having no front line to supply, and no invasion to cope with, the British home railways had an easier task than the continental systems. Nevertheless, they faced serious problems, which they mastered triumphantly. The main factor in their wartime success was the main defect of their pre-war situation. The wasteful peacetime competition, surpassing even that of the USA, ensured that there was plenty of spare capacity to cope with traffic surges. There were very few main centres in Britain which were not connected by more than one line of railway, and often there were three or four companies offering services between identical points. In peacetime this meant that traffic was spread, so that neither tracks nor trains carried anywhere near their maximum load of traffic. At the same time, interchange points between railways caused long and technically quite avoidable delays to freight traffic. The absence of freight car pooling agreements meant that a car delivering a load on to a 'foreign' railway was returned empty to the owning company rather than being employed to carry the next available load. Elimination of such uneconomic practices enabled a given stock of equipment to carry more traffic. In fact, the British railways could have easily carried much more traffic and suffered much more disturbance than they were actually called upon to accept. Another advantage was the existence of the Railway Executive Committee, established on the eve of the war, which enabled intelligent operational changes to be made by those most affected by them—the railway managers.

An early indication of the British railways' ability to find extra traffic capacity came at the very beginning. The outbreak of war

(overleaf) *Three generations of military transport serving the British front line in the Battle of Langemarck in 1917. The ammunition train is headed by a Ford rail tractor, virtually a rail-mounted motor truck*

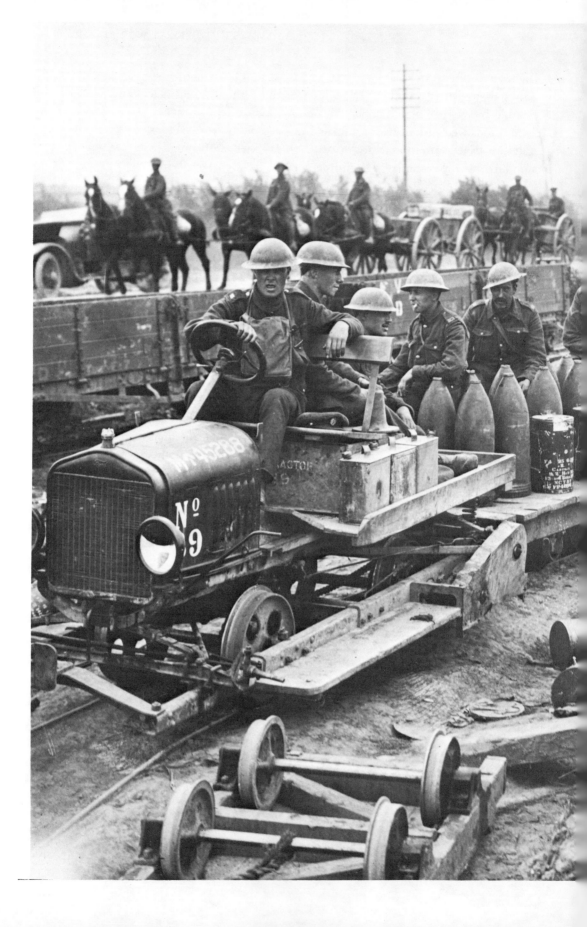

coincided with August Bank Holiday, when the Territorial Army reservists were in training at their annual camps. The extra traffic created by call-up and mobilization, as well as the despatch of the British Expeditionary Force to France, caused little congestion, even though superimposed on this already peak traffic period. Only on the London & South Western Railway, serving Southampton, were there extensive cancellations of civilian train services in order to provide capacity for the trains of troops and supplies destined for France. A number of railways did cancel some of their summer excursion trains, but this was not for long.

Although the general mobilization was ordered at midnight on Bank Holiday Sunday, 4 August, military traffic had begun before then; the Royal Navy's reserves had already been called up over the preceding weeks. When army mobilization was declared, the first phase—the reporting of reservists to their depots—was accomplished without the running of special trains. The following stage involved the despatch of the British Expeditionary Force to France, and the movement of the other mobilized units to their points of concentration. For these activities, timetables had already been prepared; as elsewhere, these included a good deal of reserve capacity so that, for example, almost all the 334 trains conveying 70,000 BEF men and their equipment to Southampton during the week of 10–17 August arrived early. By the end of August a total of 118,000 men had been conveyed to Southampton, together with their horses and guns, and there had been no serious delays to the 670 trains which had moved them. Most notably, there was excellent co-ordination between the different railway companies; a train of Scots troops could be passed from the Highland to the Caledonian, and then to the London and North Western, and finally the London & South Western Railway, with no delay at interchange points apart from the minutes needed to change engines and, sometimes, to serve refreshments. Special trains were supervised by the Deputy Assistant Director of Rail Transport at Command HQ, and it is notable that even in the first weeks of the war, when army officers tended to regard railway managers as subordinates, the Deputy Assistant Director always lent his authority to the case put by the railwaymen.

The BEF timetable envisaged trains arriving at Southampton every twelve minutes for sixteen hours of each day; if a train ran over twelve minutes late it was to lose its turn, being halted until the end of the movement. In fact no train lost its turn, and most arrived twenty or thirty minutes ahead of schedule. This was cause for much self-congratulation at the time, but the question of why it was so meritorious to arrive half an hour early but so sinful to drop twelve minutes behind remains unanswered; in a carefully arranged and intensive schedule the former might be expected to cause as much disturbance as the latter, unless all trains ran early (which is probably what happened, given the amount of recovery time incorporated in the schedules). In any case, the *Railway News* of 22 August was not slow to congratulate its readers:

'It was a wonderful achievement of toil, done in the light of flares and arc lamps. Not a man or horse was injured. Not a wagon or field piece damaged. When medals are distributed the railway workers should certainly receive them. The automatic departure of the trains was truly marvellous; they worked to a time-table, and were run with greater regularity than is the ordinary traffic of an August bank holiday. A half battalion of infantry marched up, hoisted their machine guns and water cart aboard, climbed into the waiting carriages themselves, and twenty minutes later they were off. Little more time was expended upon a squadron of cavalry or a battery of artillery, although there were horses to box and guns to mount on trucks.'

Mobilization proper took two weeks, during which over 1,400 special trains were operated. After this, although troop specials continued to run in large numbers, railway managements could relax. Although the Railway Executive protected itself with notices informing the public that services might be cancelled or delayed, the various railways adopted the prevailing 'business as usual' philosophy, restoring holiday services. Indeed summer tourist and excursion tickets, which had been withdrawn by most railways in August, were not only reinstated but allowed to continue into November. Continental services continued; the Great Eastern Railway contrived to maintain its Harwich to Hook of Holland service throughout the war. But later, in November, the railways' readiness was again tested, this time by an invasion scare which resulted in 840 special trains being ordered by the home command to move troops to the threatened east coast. For some time after this a number of empty troop trains were held in readiness for another such emergency, which might, it was felt, turn out to be more real than the first.

As the war progressed, passenger services were gradually restricted. In general, the restrictions were applied by individual railways in accordance with their own particular difficulties. The London & North Western Railway was one of the lines most heavily affected by wartime traffic and was one of the earliest to introduce service reductions. On the other hand the Great Central, the newest main line, whose competitive position had been precarious before the war, was able to attract traffic by maintaining a largely pre-war standard of service at a time when its neighbours, and especially the Midland Railway, were compelled by war demands to offer an inferior service. But the Great Central could justify this policy by the relatively small military traffic which it carried. Among the more hard-pressed lines were those providing cross-London connections. Three of these, including the partly underground Metropolitan Railway, were invaluable links, enabling the trunk railways north of the Thames to run trains direct to the southern ports. Most railways lengthened their schedules, enabling heavier trains to be run. The withdrawal of most restaurant cars had a similar aim, that of enabling more passengers to be carried per train; by the end of the war there were only fifty-two restaurant car services still running, one-seventh of the pre-war total. Sleeping cars were not so badly affected, giving some critics the opportunity to claim, quite justifiably, that they were maintained because they were a convenience to the ruling classes. This claim was met, equally justifiably, by the argument that officers and government servants who were required both to travel and to make critical decisions needed a good night's rest to function properly.

In early 1917 all railways were required to reduce their passenger services. Already, to save manpower, some stations had been closed and a few branch-line services suspended (not always unwillingly). But in 1917 the Railway Executive Committee made a determined effort to ease the transport burden by shedding passenger traffic. The coal shortage, and the need to send locomotives and rolling stock to France, was the factor determining the timing of this move. There was a surge of train cancellations and decelerations. Fares were raised by fifty per cent and most of the remaining reduced-fare tickets abolished. These moves probably reduced passenger traffic by about ten per cent, considerably less than had been hoped; passengers seemed determined to make their journeys, whatever the cost and the discomfort. Earlier, Railway Executive and government spokesmen had talked of 'joy riders' and the need to eliminate them. By the end of the war there was little joy in riding the trains, but still the passengers came. In successive years, at Easter and Christmas, announcements were made that the railways would not run extra trains and could not guarantee to carry the passengers, but still the passengers presented themselves at the stations and still the railway managements contrived to duplicate the hardest-pressed services. At the same time, on lines with the capacity to spare, summer holiday trains were run even in the last years of the war. One valued concession to passengers was the introduction of ticket interavailability; at long last, for example, the holder of a return ticket from London to Birmingham could travel out on the London & North Western and return by the Great Western.

A later commentator described the British passenger as maintaining '. . . the full privilege of democratic countries to accept nothing without a growl'. In fact the passenger did more than growl, for he often ignored instructions. In the First World War the art of public relations was in its infancy and the authorities had a false confidence in the power of exhortation. Unless they were told convincingly the reasons for a request, passengers tended to do as they pleased. Thus during night air raids, instead of lowering window blinds they preferred to raise them in order to get a better view; in the end the railways were told to switch off all train lights during a raid alarm, making blinds unnecessary.

Air raids, first by Zeppelins and later by aircraft, did little damage, but at first severely hindered railway operation. This was because the initial practice was to halt all trains during an alarm. Since a single raider could cause the alarm to be imposed over vast areas, the loss in train hours was considerable. Eventually it was agreed that trains could continue to run, but at reduced speeds. The speed reduction was not so much to soothe passengers fearful of plunging into a bomb-crater, but was intended to enable trains to run with a minimum of firing. According to service advisers, it was the opening of firebox doors, and the consequent shaft of bright light, which attracted enemy raiders, enabling them not only to attack railways but, more seriously, to use the railways as a positional guide. During the war only twenty-four railwaymen were killed by air attack, eight of them in one night of severe bombing at St Pancras Station in London.

The obviously successful manner in which the British railways co-ordinated their activities through the Railway Executive Committee, converting peacetime waste into useful wartime traffic capacity, persuaded many—railwaymen, ministers, the general public—that a post-war return to the old situation was unacceptable. The British railway amalgamation of 1923 was one result of this feeling. Nowhere was the rationalizing effect of war more obvious than in railway freight transport. Extra capacity had to be found urgently, in view of the booming war economy, military needs and the shift of coastal sea traffic to the railways. The demand soon caused a freight-car shortage, but this was remedied simply by the belated application of intelligent

The infantry living quarters of a 1915 British armoured train. Both the sides and the roof are armoured. Sliding covers block the two rows of rifle slits along each side

procedures. 'Common user' or the pooling of rolling stock, was
one such advance. As early as 1915, three railways (the Great
Eastern, Great Northern and Great Central) agreed to pool their
open cars, and in 1916 another group, including the Great
Western, London North Western and North Eastern, arranged a
similar scheme, as did the three largest Scottish companies. This
meant that a company could make use of another company's
freight car that happened to be on its tracks. It was no longer
necessary to return such vehicles empty to the owning railway.
'Number-takers' at interchange points kept a record of car
movements so that at the end of each month a settlement could
be made. In January 1917 general car pooling was introduced,
covering all companies but not all cars. At first it was only open
cars which were included, but the list was gradually extended.
However, that most damaging anachronism of British railways,
the private-owner wagon, was never included. Private cars,
totalling almost half the British car stock and belonging mainly
to the colliery companies, continued to be sent back empty to
their owners. Only in the Second World War was pooling
imposed on these vehicles too.

The second drain on car resources, as with many railways
outside Britain, was the long turnround time caused by traders'
slow loading and unloading of cars, which were often regarded
by the railways' customers as a convenient form of warehousing.
Demurrage charges were officially payable for excessive turnround time, but the railway companies had always been reluctant
to insist on these. In 1917, however, the companies no longer
feared their clients' irritation, and the Railway Executive Committee began to insist on full demurrage payments, with immediate results. Unfortunately, government departments, and
especially the military, were immune to this treatment, while
being perhaps the worst offenders. Little could be done apart
from exhortation, which did have a limited success towards the
end of the war. Another military tendency was to use railway
cars for very short distances or for very small consignments.
Little could be done to prevent a local military establishment
using a ten-ton car to carry a fifty-pound consignment, but the
'ten-mile rule' introduced in 1916 did shift the shortest-haul
traffic to horse or motor transport.

As with passenger traffic, the burdens of war were distributed
unequally. The Great Northern, with its east-coast route to the

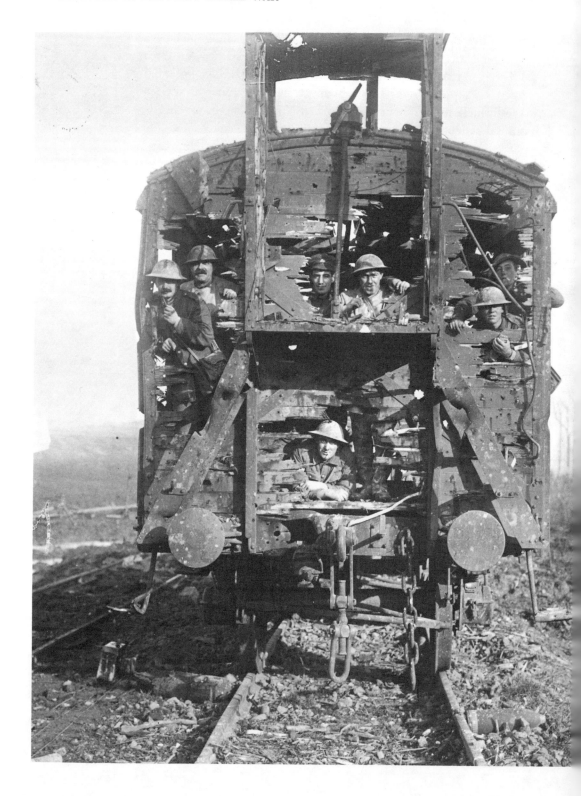

north, was overloaded by a surge of coal traffic when the New-castle–London coastal ships were removed to safer waters. The railway coped with this situation by abolishing its fast freight services and instituting a standard freight train speed of 20 mph. This, together with the slowing of the fastest passenger services, enabled a denser traffic to be carried both in terms of heavier trains and of greater line capacity.

The most celebrated of the wartime freight trains were the 'Jellicoe Specials', carrying coal from South Wales to the Grand Fleet off Scotland. By the end of the war 100 of these 600-ton trains were operated each week, covering the 375 miles from Pontypool Road to Grangemouth in under two days. There the specials transferred their coal to coastal ships. The Highland Railway, running from Perth to the very north of Scotland, was spared this extra burden which, in fact, it would never have been able to bear. For the Highland was perhaps the British railway most overtaxed by the war effort. Mainly single track, and never very prosperous, it was ill-prepared for heavy wartime traffic. It did cope with its problems, but had to borrow loco-motives from other companies to do so. It handled all kinds of naval stores, including some coal, as well as the naval passenger traffic. Much of the latter travelled in the daily 'Naval Special' in the later months of the war.

The 'Naval Special' was introduced in February 1917 to cope with the increasing (and increasingly disruptive) movement of the sailors to Scapa Flow, Invergordon and Rosyth from the southern naval depots, and on return from leave. It was the longest-distance daily train service ever operated in Britain, covering the 717 miles from the London & North Western Rail-way's London terminus at Euston to the bleak northern outpost of the Highland Railway at Thurso in twenty-one and a half hours. (On the Continent such distances were not considered especially noteworthy. In fact the inter-Allied Cherbourg to Taranto daily service, introduced in 1917 to take pressure off sea communications, ran over a 1,400-mile route.) Usually of fourteen coaches, the Naval Special made a good speed on its southern segment but toiled through the Scottish Highlands at an average of about 25 mph. Although its users could crawl out of

British soldiers pose for a photograph in a shell-torn freight car standing in a much-fought-over area near Beaucourt. Although the damage appears to be devastating, this car would have been easily repaired

their compartments at dawn to refresh themselves from tea trolleys organized by women's voluntary organizations, it probably fully deserved its nickname of 'Misery Special'. The southbound service, although identical, was a happier train, for obvious reasons. In early 1918 the northbound train was snowed-up for a week near Thurso; long before it was dug out the sailors had finished the remaining miles of their journey on foot. Other naval specials ran on to the Highland Railway from Portsmouth and Plymouth, but these were not regular daily services. Most sailors travelling from Plymouth to Scotland changed onto the Naval Special at Crewe.

The railways had expected that wartime operation would lead to financial loss, and the terms on which they placed themselves under government control through the Railway Executive Council were designed to protect them against this. However, these terms had the reverse effect, preventing them making excess profits. Briefly, the government guaranteed them their pre-war net revenue. With this guarantee, the railways were willing enough to agree to carry government traffic free, which meant that they could not profit when such traffic reached unexpectedly high levels. Later in the war the government relented enough to make extra payments to cover the higher wages needed to cope with general inflation and to partly cover deferred maintenance. When the war ended, however, there were high and justified claims outstanding for deferred maintenance and the government, disregarding wartime understandings, refused to pay up. It was only after much manoeuvring, appeals to public opinion and special commissions, that a compromise was reached, the railways accepting compensation which was probably below that to which in justice they were entitled.

Dirty equipment, and the continued use of obsolete equipment because of the changeover to munitions production of so many railway works, were two features of the wartime face of Britain's railways. Another was the increasing use of female labour. Confined before the war to secretarial, catering and some cleaning services, female labour spread into most railway trades with the exception of some operating grades, such as enginemen. By their standards of that time, the railway unions reacted generously to this situation, accepting women workers on condition that they were discharged at the end of the war and that they received the

The British railways' workshops, well-equipped and well-run, were largely transferred to war production in both world wars. Here, newly-recruited women assemble shell fuses at the Lancashire & Yorkshire Railway's Horwich workshops in 1915

minimum wage; the possibility of a woman receiving more than a man in the same job was outrageously unacceptable. Women porters became an everyday sight at the main stations, but although an attempt was made to use women in signal cabins they could do little to replace the more highly skilled men who had left for the forces in 1914. By the end of the war 68,000 women were serving on the railways. On the other hand, almost one-third (184,500) of the 1914 male staff had joined the forces. Of these 184,500 less than a quarter served in the railway battalions, and 21,500 were killed. As in other countries, Britain did little in the early weeks of the war to conserve her trained railway specialists. In a fit of war-losing patriotism many highly experienced men volunteered for service in 1914, almost all of them being drafted to the infantry. Later in the war skilled railwaymen, when called up at all, were usually sent to railway battalions or other arms, where proper use could be made of their qualifications. But the 1914 patriots soldiered on in the infantry.

Although after the war several of the American railroad companies published self-congratulatory accounts of their war-time triumphs, the reality was rather different. Put briefly, the role of the companies after the American entry into the war in 1917 was to do as they were told, since they were obviously incapable of delivering the goods if left on their own. As in the Civil War, railroad managements, even if they wished to do so, could not place the general interest before the interest of their shareholders. This meant, in effect, that the USA, so long as the companies maintained their independence, could never have a true railway system, only a collection of enterprises which might or might not co-operate and co-ordinate their activities. Since nationalization was very much feared by the companies, it was embarrassing that during the years of government control over the railroads there were real improvements in efficiency; this is probably why objective histories of this period are so rare.

Just as in the early days of the Civil War railroad managements met and promised self-sacrificing support for the war effort, so in April 1917 did the railroad presidents meet in Washington and pass a resolution in similar terms, pledging '. . . that during the present war they will co-ordinate their operations in a continental railway system, merging during such period all their merely individual and competitive activities in the effort to produce a maximum of national transportation efficiency. . . .' For that time, this was a remarkable admission of the short-comings of the competitive system and there seems no reason to doubt the sincerity of those who made it. But they must surely have known that what they were proposing was against the law; the Sherman Anti Trust Act and the Interstate Commerce Act had been designed precisely to ensure that individual and competitive activities should not be weakened. Indeed, in November 1917, after five months of war, the Attorney-General refused on these grounds to give his approval to a scheme whereby the different railroads would co-ordinate their activities west of Pittsburgh.

Even before America declared war the railroads, conscious of the bad reputation they had earned in the Spanish–American War, when they had plainly put their own profits before anything else, had joined together to try and find ways of co-ordinating their work. Because of anti-trust legislation, and because their first responsibility had to be towards their shareholders, they had not done much more than decide what the most pressing problems would be. However, during the Mexican crisis of 1915, they had succeeded in transporting the National Guard troops to the Mexican frontier in an unexpectedly efficient and rapid manner. After 1916 the president of the Baltimore & Ohio Railroad, Daniel Willard, was the transportation member of the Advisory Commission of the Council of National Defense, and he had quietly made contacts with fellow railroad presidents to work out what should be done in case of war. The April 1917 meeting in Washington of the fifty-one railroad presidents was at Willard's initiative; he was also the inspiration behind the resolution which they passed and their decision to set up a Railroads' War Board.

The War Board, under the chairmanship of the Southern Railway president, did what it could during 1917 to solve the problem of carrying a rapidly increasing traffic to the Atlantic ports. In fact, this traffic had begun to grow in 1915, when the belligerents of Europe turned to the USA for supplies. Whereas in the first months of 1915 the railroads had about 300,000 surplus freight cars, by the end of 1916 there was a shortage of about 115,000 (equivalent to a freight train 850 miles long). This freight-car shortage meant that shipments had to wait for ever-increasing periods before being loaded, and when America entered the war this could no longer be tolerated by the army, navy or any other department. A system of 'priority tags' was introduced, but as railroad freight agents tended to distribute these as favours to clients (four-fifths of the shipments were provided with these tags), it was soon seen that they were of very little value. There was little attempt at overall planning—indeed there could not be, since there was nobody with the power to enforce decisions. The approaches to the eastern ports and the ports themselves were clogged with traffic, so that the freight-car shortage became even more acute as whole trainloads waited for days or weeks to be unloaded. Many cases of inane operation were witnessed. Perhaps the most stupendous of these was when the government decided to build new shipyards on a swamp near Philadelphia. Trainloads of building supplies, all with top priority, were rushed to the site before there were any facilities to unload them; within a few weeks these thousands of unloaded freight cars were blocking sidings and yards over a large area of eastern Pennsylvania.

It was only at the end of November 1917, when the situation

of the eastern railroads was desperate, that the Railroads' War Board took what it called 'revolutionary measures'. These in fact were the kind of decisions which the railways of continental Europe had envisaged well before the outbreak of war. They included the diversion of east to west traffic to lines north and south of Pittsburgh, thereby relieving the congestion of the Pittsburgh Division of the Pennsylvania Railroad; the zoning of coal deliveries to avoid cross-hauls (that is, coal shipments moving in both directions between two regions); a car pool for open-top vehicles; the standardization of a slow speed for freight trains so that all trains would be heavy and slow, without fast freights disturbing the movement pattern; the transfer of loco-motives from one railway with excess stock to another, more hard-pressed line; and the treatment of parallel single-track routes of competing railroads as a double-track system for operational purposes. All these measures, though somewhat tardy, were very useful. But there were some additional measures which needed to be taken, but which were beyond the powers of the War Board. One of these would have been to eliminate excessively long routing of freight. The longstanding tradition whereby a railroad so routed a shipment as to produce the maximum mileage, and hence revenue, over its own tracks meant that freight did not travel by the shortest routes between two points. Such a practice meant that shipments were slower and, more important, more precious car-miles and locomotive-miles were required. But exhortations had little effect on this practice. After all, the first duty of a railroad was to make maximum profits for its shareholders.

Labour unrest during 1917, largely stimulated by the out-pacing of railway wage rates by those of the new war industries, made matters worse. And then, at the end of 1917, the blizzards came. Although railroad managements and workers made great, often heroic, efforts to carry on, it was clear that the railroad crisis was poised on the edge of a railroad catastrophe—a com-plete stoppage which might take weeks to sort out. On 28 Decem-ber 1917 the government took control of the railroads '. . . not because of any dereliction or failure on their part', as President Wilson put it, 'but only because there were some things which the government can do and private management cannot'.

It was not until 1920 that the railroads were handed back to their owners. In the meantime, some rationality was brought into their operation, so that by the end of the war they were coping very well with the vastly increased traffic. Government control did not, however, do anything to improve the long-term prospects of the US railroads. Throughout 1918 the government's Director-General of Railroads was William McAdoo, who had the advantage of not being a railroadman while having railroad associations. A financier and lawyer, he had been responsible for the building of the railroad tunnels under the Hudson River at New York. Under him there grew up the United States Railroad Administration (USRA), which for a few months did seem to create a true unified railroad network, and which consisted largely of railroaders chosen for their ability to take a broad view of the situation.

The first task for the USRA was to impose order on the chaos resulting from the congestion of the eastern railroads. In some places cars were sent forward quite irrespective of any priority which they might have; those which could be extricated first were despatched first, which in itself was a principle which made the task much easier. Eventually the priority system was abandoned in favour of stricter controls over shipments and routing. Federal managers replaced an increasing number of railroad managers as time passed, and the nation's railroads were grouped into three administrative regions, namely the Eastern, Southern and Western. It was the Eastern region that was the most critical, and McAdoo appointed his friend Alfred Smith to take charge of it. Smith was formerly of the New York Central Railroad, so his appointment created considerable resentment in the rival Pennsylvania Railroad, whose officials complained that Smith was intentionally diverting traffic away from their lines. This, in fact, was quite true, for the Pennsylvania was the most congested of all lines and there could be no hope of solving the transport problem without diverting its traffic to parallel lines—and thus, in some cases, to the New York Central.

Federal control gave the railroads advantages which they could not have enjoyed under private control. They were no longer subject to the anti-trust laws, so could pool their services without restriction. They had direct access through McAdoo to the President. They could get priority treatment for their own material needs. They could forget about profit and loss, knowing that the government would always provide enough money to keep the railroads running. And they could obtain deferment of conscription for their most skilled and essential employees.

Interestingly enough, one of the first successes of the Railroad Administration was obtained not by using its power, but by exhortation. An intense publicity campaign to persuade shippers to load freight cars more rationally, and to make full use of the available space, resulted in an increase of two tons in the average load of a freight car; this alone represented a ten per cent increase in carrying capacity. Increases of demurrage charges had a similar effect. Clients who failed to unload their cars soon enough now faced quite crippling penalties, as much as ten dollars a day for a car detained more than seven days. The institution of 'sailing day discipline' for less-than-carload shipments was another useful saver of freight-car miles; small shipments were held for despatch on certain days of the week only, thus ensuring that enough cargo would accumulate to properly fill the freight cars.

Because the 3,400 locomotives which the railroads had ordered for delivery in 1918 were not received (the manufacturers having given priority to locomotives ordered by France and Russia), the American railroads also faced a severe locomotive shortage. The USRA alleviated this by leasing 200 locomotives built for Russia but undelivered because of the Russian Revolution, as well as 135 built for France but not yet required. About 200 other locomotives were transferred from the less busy to the overloaded railroads. Then 1,930 locomotives and 10,000 freight cars were ordered by the USRA. The locomotives were built to standard USRA designs and many survived until the last days of American steam traction. By the end of the war the railroads had over a thousand locomotives in reserve, compared to December 1917, when there was no reserve at all. This improvement was only partly due to the delivery of USRA locomotives; more important was the better average condition of the locomotives, and the better use made of them. The Railroad Administration's largely successful effort to send freight by the shortest route, and to plan the traffic flows so as to avoid delays, meant that fewer locomotives were required for the same traffic.

With over six million troops carried in the ten months between government takeover and the Armistice, it was necessary to discourage passenger travel. Because in peacetime so many passenger services were run for competitive reasons rather than for real need, it was not difficult to reduce the number of trains.

Between big cities it was quite normal to have several competing railroads providing services, and many of these tended to be non-stop. By cutting out many of these trains and by compelling the remainder to make more intermediate stops, a reasonable service could still be provided at a considerable saving in train-miles. Passenger tickets became valid for all alternative routes. In the cities, where each railroad had its own ticket office, a single combined office was usually established. Apart from economizing in staff this also meant that a passenger who failed to get the reservation he needed on one railroad no longer had to go to another office to see what another company could offer. A number of Pullman and dining cars were taken out of normal service and a few lightly used trains were removed from the timetables. Thus although passenger traffic increased by eight per cent in 1918, there was at the same time a reduction of ten per cent in passenger services. There could hardly have been a clearer example of the cost of pre-war competition.

Yet when the railroads were returned to private ownership in 1920 these lessons were disregarded. Pooling arrangements ended. Roundabout freight routing returned. Passenger ticket offices multiplied in the big cities. Locomotives were built in small batches to suit each individual railroad. In retrospect, it would seem that only one legacy of the USRA was long-lasting; railroad managements determined that they would never again get themselves into a situation where the government had no alternative but to take control. With this objective, the railroads did come together to work out how they could properly coordinate their activities in a future war. As it turned out, they were successful in this, and in the Second World War they remained in private control.

Chapter 6

Second World War and After

The belief that a philosophy which has worked well in the past should be good enough for the future is a traditional guide to conduct for railway managements. It is a philosophy which is not unknown, either, in war ministries. So it is hardly surprising that in the inter-war years the experiences of the First World War determined the expectations of how the railways should be managed in a future conflict. However, there was one novelty: the anticipation of air attack. In the 1930s both civilian populations and military planners expected that, a few hours after a declaration of war, skies would be blackened by hordes of aircraft hurling high explosives, incendiaries and poison gases on to fearful cities.

There was a minor dress rehearsal for 1939 at the time of the Munich crisis of 1938. In Britain, for a few days, enough extra trains were run to equal the summer holiday peak. This emergency performance by the British companies was carefully noted in other countries. In Soviet Russia, where both the railway authorities and the military were conscious that war was not far off, one railway journal gave a fairly detailed description of the events in London. It began with a predictably acid interpretation of the situation:

'At the end of September, largely to scare the "average Englishman", trenches for underground gas shelters were dug in the London parks. People queued in the streets for gas-

September 3, 1939—Britain goes to war, by rail

masks. . . . At the London stations during those days naval reservists stormed the trains, together with frightened inhabitants who were taking their families from London to areas safer from air attack.'

After thus suitably setting the scene, and adding that the trains to the Channel ports were packed with apprehensive young Frenchmen called up for the army, Italian waiters from London restaurants hurrying home, and hordes of German women who had worked as domestic servants in London returning to their families, the article continued with a detailed and instructive account of how the British government had dealt with the evacuation of children from London:

'Schoolchildren had to turn up in good order, in entire classes or groups under the supervision of teachers. At the stations all evacuees were to receive free railway tickets. They were to be carried by rail 50–80 km from the capital in various directions. . . . In the event of damage to the railway lines by bombing it was anticipated that supplementary use would be made of road transport and also of river and canal steamers. . . . The evacuation of London was begun with the despatch of 4·5 thousand children. However it was later stopped and from 4 October the "refugees" began to return to town. . . .'

If September 1938 was an anticlimax for British railways, September 1939 also had an air of unreality, because the anticipated bombers did not materialize. In the meantime the railways had studied the threat. Shortage of funds (or, more accurately, a natural preference to wait for government financial support) had meant that not much had been done, but some air raid shelters were built, some wooden signal boxes at key junctions were replaced by stronger brick-built structures, and emergency communications systems were devised. Locomotives were provided with gas-detector panels for dealing with gas attacks on trains; a change of colour would indicate that the train had passed through a cloud of gas and its crew would thereupon take it to the nearest decontamination yard.

Well before the war the railway companies had fitted out ambulance trains, which were stationed in convenient sidings, awaiting a declaration of hostilities. Their task, which was carried out smartly in September, was the removal of hospital patients from London and other cities threatened by bombing.

Evacuation of schoolchildren from London and other cities followed. This went very smoothly, thanks to the abundant rolling stock traditionally kept in service for the summer holiday peak traffic. Many of these children went to south coast resorts, and had to be re-evacuated the following year, or in 1944 when the flying bombs again made the south unsafe. There were plans in 1941 for the evacuation of areas threatened by invasion, involving almost 1,000 extra trains in four days. These plans were never needed and were somewhat unwarlike, intended for women and children rather than key industries and their workers.

Hundreds of thousands of bewildered and disconsolate soldiers poured into England's south-eastern ports after their evacuation from Dunkirk in 1940. Here, French soldiers arrive at Margate

Apart from the new element of air attack, 1939 was not unlike 1914 for the British railways, with the same heavy troop traffic to France through the southern ports, and the supervision by a Railway Executive modelled on that of 1914. 1940, however, did not resemble 1915; Dunkirk and the Battle of Britain made that year unique.

The sudden, urgent and intense traffic which presented itself as British and Allied troops arrived at the Channel ports from Dunkirk was handled so admirably that it raises the question of whether long-term planning of military rail movements serves any real purpose. What enabled the British railways, and especially the Southern Railway, to cope with this emergency was not planning, of which there was none, but the good will and hard work of all railwaymen (there seems to have been only one dispute about overtime during the evacuation), the availability at key points of railway officials who were both willing to take responsibility for quick decisions and whose knowledge of railway conditions ensured that those decisions would be the best possible, and the existence on the railways of easily utilizable excess capacity. In this last aspect the speed with which the other three railway companies assembled trains and sent them to the Southern Railway was especially important; rapid availability of empty rolling stock was the key factor of the success, since normal train services were maintained except around Redhill and Dover.

The arriving troops were sent in all directions. Some were ordered to remain in the south and so did not need long-distance trains. French troops had to be sent to the south-west for re-embarkation. But most went north, and most of these did not pass through London. The junction at Redhill, near London, became the key to the control and movement of the week-long procession of special trains. An awkward layout, necessitating reversals, did not prove an insuperable obstacle to speedy and efficient operation. More difficulty was experienced on the locomotive side, for it was at Redhill that engines were changed. The station's locomotive depot was not designed to cope with the hundreds of locomotives that arrived there, requiring fuelling, turning and servicing. At one point locomotive water ran short and towards the end of the evacuation so many locomotives had had their smokeboxes and grates cleaned that there was an accumulation of about 300 tons of ash hampering work in the depot. Some locomotives had to be sent to other depots to take on coal, either to ease congestion or to reduce the demand on the local coal stock. Despite all these difficulties, there seem to have been no instances of locomotive shortage causing serious hold-ups.

No doubt the experience of the Southern Railway, predominantly a passenger railway, in handling peacetime holiday and peak traffic was an excellent preparation for its wartime trials. Probably, too, the density and complexity of its train services gave the management useful experience for coping with bomb damage. Heavy bombing started in 1940 and affected all four railway companies, although, again, it was the Southern which was most damaged. Hundreds of bombs were dropped on railway property, often causing hold-ups of several days. Railwaymen, especially those working in large stations and yards, were at considerable risk; during the war, about 400 were killed on duty. Large numbers had been trained on a voluntary basis in firefighting, and this training would seem, in retrospect, to have been one of the decisive factors enabling the railways to survive the attack and continue to meet the demands made upon them. Some of the London termini were out of action for a day or two, typically because of the collapse of bridges or arches. On one occasion London's Waterloo Station continued to operate trains with all signalling out of action; a devoted band of amateurs continued to flag trains in and out over the few passable tracks. In early May of 1941 seven of the London termini (Waterloo, Victoria, Charing Cross, Cannon Street, London Bridge, King's Cross and St Pancras) were out of action following bomb damage; on this occasion it was a week before Waterloo could bring half its tracks back into service, and almost a month before service was completely restored.

The flying bomb attacks of 1944 were an unexpected threat, and therefore depressing for morale. But railwaymen made the same kind of all-out effort to cope that they had made in 1940 and 1941. It is significant that the unaimed flying bomb of 1944 was as likely to cause serious railway damage as the aimed bomb of 1940.

The Southern Railway, and to a lesser extent the London & North Eastern, were troubled in the first half of the war by

(overleaf) *In Britain, as in Germany, the old arched iron roofs of large stations stood up well to bombing, although railway tracks were sometimes out of action for several weeks. This is York station after it was bombed in July 1942*

attacks on their trains in the countryside, with locomotives as prime targets. Several enginemen were killed, and one German aircraft, which incautiously flew over the locomotive it had been cannonading, was brought down when the boiler blew up beneath it. Sometimes trains took refuge in tunnels, or made sudden changes of speed in order to make the enemy's aim more difficult. There were a handful of cases in which passenger trains plunged into bomb craters, but as speeds were usually low the number of deaths was quite small. Throughout Britain, trains were blacked-out at night. In the early period light bulbs were painted dark blue, giving just sufficient light to enable passengers to avoid sitting down on occupied seats. Blinds were drawn and the outer margins of the windows painted black. Station illumination was out of the question; a white line painted on the platform edge was intended to show passengers where to alight. This white line, however, was less successful in showing passengers where not to alight. The most spectacular inadvertent jump was made by a passenger in a long train that stopped at Bath with its rear projecting beyond the platform end; this gentleman stepped out of the train on to the parapet of the bridge on which his vehicle was standing, plunged into the River Avon far below, and lived to tell the tale.

Possessing some of the finest engineering works in the country, the railway companies were also soon involved in the manufacture of weapons, including aircraft, tanks and small ships. Meanwhile, locomotive production slowed down. Early in the war, as in 1914, the railways gave up some of their locomotives for government service, and these included some of the veteran Great Western 0-6-0 type sent abroad in the First World War. Many of the latter, as well as some diesel locomotives, were lost when France fell. At home, locomotive production was concentrated on the LMS Railway's design of 2-8-0 freight locomotive, which was built in several workshops. The government-imposed emphasis on freight locomotives was presumably why, in 1941, the new streamlined passenger locomotives of the Southern Railway's 'Merchant Navy' class were officially described as 'air-smoothed mixed traffic engines'.

Several railway workshops also built armoured trains. These took a classical form, with the heavily armoured locomotive in the centre and armoured gun platforms at each end. The miniature pleasure railway centred on Hythe in Sussex also had its

During the invasion threat of 1940 a number of armoured trains were assembled to help defend the British coast. This is the locomotive of one of them, camouflaged and with armour plating for the crew

coastal armoured train. In the event, these armoured trains served little practical purpose, being intended for use on coastal lines during an invasion. On the Southern Railway, at Dover, rail-mounted 9·2-inch guns were hauled periodically to one or another gun siding, moored to hawsers, and used to bombard the French coast in the hope of hitting the corresponding German guns near Calais. By 1943 invasion seemed unlikely, and the armoured trains ceased their slow patrol up and down coastal lines. Earlier, the special measures taken to save locomotives in case of invasion had been relaxed. Locomotives at Ramsgate, on the south-eastern coast, for example, were no longer kept in steam ready for a quick getaway, and locomotives stationed at Dundee

193

on the east coast were no longer withdrawn each night inland to Perth. But the railway guns at Dover kept firing until 1944.

Throughout most of the railway age it had been the Prussians, and then the Germans, who had been leaders in the application of railways to warfare. But despite careful planning there was one problem which they had never quite solved—the gap between the supply railhead and their advancing troops. In the wars against Austria, Imperial France and Republican France, their leading troops had advanced so fast that the horse transport on which they relied to bring their supplies up to the fighting front was outdistanced. In 1866 and 1870 they won their wars in spite of this, but in 1914 they lost the Battle of the Marne partly for supply reasons. With the advent of practical motor transport, they might have been expected to have solved this problem by 1939. Hitler seems to have thought they had, but he was wrong.

In his enthusiasm for the automobile and the *autobahn*, Hitler had rather neglected his railways, and only a few divisions were fully motorized when he went to war. Driving through Belgium, his troops discovered that their motor transport was insufficient and that the Belgian railways had been effectively put out of action. The German railway troops, as in 1914, were too few to put things right in time, so German civilian motor trucks were commandeered in large numbers, with predictable effects on German economic life. In the French campaign the motorized troops went so fast that they not only outran their motor supply services but also the non-motorized infantry. It was only the immediate French surrender which saved them from the need to halt and consolidate.

Earlier, against Poland, these deficiencies had not shown themselves so obviously. With what in retrospect seems uncharacteristic foresight, the German railway troops were intensively employed to raise the standards of the railways in German-occupied Poland for the campaign against Russia. By summer 1941 it was calculated that the Polish railways would be able to pass up to 420 daily trains on the east–west axis. Since the German army sent into Russia was to exceed three million men, with hundreds of thousands of horses, this capacity was vital. However, inside Russia railway transport was expected to play a relatively minor role in the two southernmost prongs of the German attack, though the northern prong, against Leningrad, was to be somewhat more rail-oriented. In any case, each of the army groups involved had only one line of railway to supply it during the advance; motor transport, it was hoped, would do the rest.

In practice, though, motor transport could do little better than horses. Because of the poor Russian roads, speeds were low and fuel consumption high, so that the effective range of road transport was only about sixty miles. This meant that an unanticipated burden was laid on rail transport, which was already having problems. The Russians in their retreat had taken the best locomotives with them, and sabotaged the others. Very little rolling stock had been left behind—most of it had been used to evacuate people and plant. In order to obtain stock, the German command adopted the rather desperate expedient of planning troop advances and air attacks with a view to cutting lines before the Russians could take away their railway cars. Meanwhile the motorized troops were pushing ahead, having priority for fuel supplies and for motor trucks over the remaining troops. These included the railway troops, who were allowed only some captured and rather ineffective British and French vehicles. When fuel supplies allowed, the railway troops followed the advanced troops in these trucks; in other words, they advanced ahead of the bulk of the infantry, before occupied territory was properly consolidated. This, together with the tendency of motorized offensives to follow roads, not railways, meant that when railway troops arrived at the railway facilities they were intended to restore they found them still firmly in the hands of the Russians. Nevertheless, on the Northern Front the railway troops managed to re-gauge and repair one through track for 300 miles in the first month of the campaign. But even so, line capacity was only about one-tenth of that which was needed. Shortage of rolling stock was worsened by the time spent at break-of-gauge points. Some trains, for one reason or another, never arrived. So the armoured troops, having arrived at the outskirts of Leningrad, were obliged to postpone their final attack on that city because of supply difficulties. Similarly, the failure of fuel trains to reach Guderian's armour was a main cause of the failure to capture Moscow. Later, in the winter of 1941, it was the railways' inability to deliver anti-freeze that led to the disintegration of the German motorized units.

Partisan attacks made the situation worse. Apart from the line blockages caused by derailments, lack of security meant that rail-heads could not be advanced as fast as was desirable. There were

*A Soviet freight locomotive in German hands during the Second World War.
Although it carries German insignia, it will be of little service, for its
cylinders have been blown off by Russian demolition charges*

equipment difficulties too. The few repairable Russian locomotives could not be easily converted to work on the re-gauged
lines, while the German locomotives brought in to the area of
operations were too heavy for many sections. Also, the German
machines were less well protected against the winter cold; burst
pipes incapacitated many of them. Lack of locomotive water,
especially in the winter months, caused great difficulty, too;
eventually, condensing apparatus identical to that designed
originally by German firms for the USSR in the 1930s was
fitted to new German war-service locomotives. While German
railway troops and imported civilian railwaymen struggled with
problems that often proved insuperable, the Nazi commanders
blamed each other for the chaos. Units were accused, sometimes
correctly, of commandeering supply trains destined for other
units. The Luftwaffe command, never on good terms with the

other arms, was accused of putting guards on its trains not for defence against partisans but for defence against Germans.

Thus it was the German communications which failed in the Russian campaign, whereas Hitler had counted on a Russian railway breakdown. In fact the Russian railways worked quite well, all through the war. They were better prepared for war than the German railways; with its breakneck industrialization, unexpected reversals of plans and fortunes, sudden deaths and strict centralized control, Russia of the 1930s was a useful experience for railwaymen about to enter a savage war. In general, the Russian railways demonstrated the truth of the mid-nineteenth-century view that railway transport strengthened the attacked rather than the attacker, a view that became unfashionable after the Franco–Prussian War. As the German supply lines were precariously extended, the Russian railways contracted, while evacuated locomotives and stock meant that the amount of equipment per mile increased. In 1943, for example, the Russian railway mileage had decreased by forty per cent, but the locomotive stock by only fifteen per cent. At the same time, because of reduced territory and the restriction of services, there was a halving of traffic.

Nevertheless, even with these advantages, the achievement of the Soviet railways was great. The wholesale evacuation of factory plant and workers from threatened western areas to the east was the first great success, carried out under air bombardment and during a period of heavy military traffic. Line capacity, throughout the war, was the main bottleneck, at times alleviated by permissive working with trains following each other almost nose to tail.

The railways played a key role in the defence of both Moscow and Leningrad. The situation at Moscow provided a reflection of the Franco–Prussian War in one way. In the latter, the French had found that the convergence of their main lines on Paris, with little provision for exchanging trains from one main line to another, was a great handicap which they remedied before the First World War with the *Grande Ceinture*, a peripheral line around the outskirts of Paris. At Moscow in 1941 there existed a newly built *ceinture*, the Moscow Belt Railway, and it was this which, after all but four of the lines radiating from the capital had been cut by the Germans, received, unloaded and returned the troop trains from the east. At Leningrad the railways were

A Soviet locomotive as the German railway troops found it at Novosokolniki in 1943. A demolition charge in the firebox has ensured that it will never be of use to its captors

unable to save the lives of those fated to die from starvation, but the city was never entirely cut off from outside supplies. Even when all the railway lines were cut, motor transport operated over the frozen Lake Ladoga to meet trains arriving on the opposite shore. In the winter of 1942–43, perhaps remembering the epic of Lake Baikal in the Russo–Japanese War, a line was actually laid across Lake Ladoga; however it was never used because on the verge of completion it was superseded by a railway built around the recently reconquered southern tip of the lake. On this latter line trains moved to the city at night, one behind the other, and returned the following night; daytime operation was impossible because the line was well within German artillery range.

Acts of heroism by Soviet railwaymen became almost a norm

rather than an exception. Nevertheless, the invasion came at a time when a substantial proportion of the population would have welcomed defeat for the Soviet regime. The pre-war purges had weeded out the loyal rather than the disloyal, it seemed, and the railway staff were quite typical in this respect. For this reason the extension of martial law to the railways was soon followed by firing squads for railwaymen who failed to do their job to the required standard. Again, no doubt, the good suffered with the bad and it is quite likely that the railwaymen would have performed better without this particular kind of incentive. Realizing, perhaps, that carrots, even tasteless carrots, were better than sticks, in 1943 the government authorized the striking of medals for railwaymen so that, for example, a railway worker who continued to issue documents in quintuplicate under bombardment could receive the Distinguished Railway Clerk medal.

When the Red Army advanced it was the turn of the Russian railway troops to reconstruct and re-gauge; many much-fought-over lines were re-gauged several times by each combatant. German destruction was very thorough and usually the Russian troops restored only one track of double-track main lines. In the advance through Poland and Germany existing main lines were often converted to the Russian gauge; it was a Russian locomotive and a Russian train which took Stalin to the Potsdam Conference in 1945.

During the war about 4,500 miles of new track were laid. Some of this had great strategic importance. A 600-mile north–south line along the Volga from Kazan to Stalingrad was finished in 1944, while a 210-mile line from Astrakhan to Kizliar enabled the north Caucasus to be supplied even after the Germans had cut the railway from the north. There was also a line connecting the southern portions of the Murmansk and Archangel lines. These had been of great importance during the First World War for passing supplies to Russia from the west, and they played a similar, but enlarged, role in the Second World War. The connecting line made it possible to continue to unload Allied ships at Murmansk even after the Germans had cut the Murmansk line near Leningrad.

A surer link between Russia and the west was the 865-mile Trans-Iranian Railway from the Persian Gulf to the Caspian Sea. This line, built before the war, was taken over by the British and Russians in 1941. The British operated the lines south of Teheran, and the Russians looked after the sections from Teheran to the Caspian Sea. The Russians, at first, relied on the Railway's existing equipment and had some difficulty in handling the traffic; for a whole week, in one difficult period, traffic was brought to a complete halt on the Anglo-American section to enable the Russians to clear their blockages. The British handed over to the Americans in 1944, having in the meantime developed the line with new passing loops, imported equipment, and a new port and connecting railway at Khoramshahr. The British railway troops found that this route, with its desert and mountain sections, was the most difficult they were called upon to operate. Water was often scarce and usually corrosive, and temperatures were such that locomotive injectors often failed and locomotive men sometimes collapsed from heat-stroke. Trains were powered by three locomotives on the steepest sections, and armed guards and interpreters were carried to deal with bandits. Conditions became a little easier after American equipment arrived; diesel locomotives were especially welcome for tunnel work, where near-asphyxiation was the frequent lot of crews of hard-working steam locomotives. The Trans-Iranian was perhaps the best known of the war's great supply railways, and it certainly did much to help the Russians to meet the German onslaught. The Burma–Siam Railway, with its Bridge on the River Kwai, was most celebrated for the lethal conditions in which it was built by prisoner-of-war labour; it had little effect on the fortunes of Japanese troops fighting in Burma because it was never completed as intended.

In the last years of the war the German railways endured some of the heaviest bombing attacks ever directed against railways, although possibly not the most damaging. The Anglo-American air assault was made from a great height, and largely at night. Where railway lines were hit it was usually by chance, except when large stations and marshalling yards were the target, in which case a small proportion of the many heavy bombs did find some kind of mark. Saturation bombing was extremely damaging to railway operations when it was repeated day after day, because although repairs were usually completed rapidly, a succession of raids could severely disorganize traffic. Moreover the work capacity of railwaymen was sapped by constant alerts, lack of sleep, and the knowledge that bombs aimed at the railway might well kill their families. The most serious damage was that caused to signalling installations, which were hard to replace even though the railways did have a few emergency mobile signal frames installed in converted freight cars.

Allied attempts to 'knock out' specific lines were usually less successful than the bomber crews or their commanders believed. The saga of the railway viaduct at Bielefeld on the German side was rather like that of HMS *Ark Royal* on the British. This vital bridge, linking the North Sea ports with the Ruhr, was bombed, first by British and then by American bombers, for four years. It was several times thought to have been wrecked, but in fact it was only in 1945, when bombs were so big that a near miss could be damaging, that one of its piers was fatally undermined. By that time the Germans had built a concealed by-pass line for just such an eventuality, and rail traffic hardly faltered.

The first crisis for German railways came in 1942, when a large number of vital locomotives, as well as railwaymen, had been sent to Russia. Those locomotives that did return were often unusable because of damage incurred in the Russian winter. Special locomotive repair measures had to be taken, while the construction of new locomotives was accelerated by assembly-line techniques and concentration on just one type; in 1943, with only the *Kriegslok* being built, no fewer than 5,243 locomotives were produced. In 1944, with the saturation air raids, the railways once more fell on bad times, and never recovered until after the war. In the final year of the conflict they provided the most serious bottleneck in the whole Nazi economy. The Nazi leadership never seemed to understand transport problems. Until the last days, railway operation, difficult in any case, was needlessly disturbed by the special trains in which Nazi dignitaries liked to cruise, while in the winter of 1944–45 local *gauleiters* would stop coal trains passing through their domains and unload the contents for their own purposes.

Oil shortages rendered useless the stock of diesel railcars in which the German railways had invested heavily in the 1930s. The need to use brown coal and briquettes as an *ersatz* fuel reduced locomotive efficiency by as much as a half, often necessitating two locomotives instead of one, and two firemen instead of one on each locomotive. Another shortage was creosote, so

(overleaf) *The famous railway bridge across the Rhine at Remagen, as it was when it was captured, damaged but usable, by American armoured troops advancing into Germany*

new cross-ties were soaked in zinc chloride, a salt which was only half as effective. The cross-ties themselves were of smaller cross-section, to enable smaller and younger trees to be used. Göring's suggestion that to save steel locomotives might be built of concrete was never taken seriously.

Thanks to the high pre-war standards of maintenance, much of the effect of material shortages was delayed. Bridges were often left unpainted during the war, but emerged in fine condition. Steel shortage meant that standards of permissible rail wear were considerably relaxed, but by the end of the war there was only a general 80 km/h (50 mph) speed limit. The standard war locomotive was basically a peacetime design, but in order to save steel and scarce metals, and to reduce the man-hours required as well as to permit the widespread use of unskilled forced labour, the type was modified into the very austere but highly successful *Kriegslok*. This required about 8,000 man-hours to build compared with the 22,000 of its more sophisticated predecessor. Designed with Russia in mind, it had a cab that was not only completely closed in but also accommodated two bunks for the crew.

Although the *Kriegslok* was by far the most numerous of the war-service locomotives, corresponding locomotives were built in the USA and Britain. In Britain locomotive construction was concentrated on an existing design of freight locomotive, the '8F' 2-8-0, which was built both for the home railways and for use overseas. The export units went to the Middle East. Later the British built the 'Austerity' locomotive, using the same 2-8-0 wheel arrangement, but designed to make the least possible use of scarce materials and to be suitable for the railways of Europe, which, it was expected, would be in a poorly maintained state. A simple 'Austerity' shunting locomotive was also designed, based on a pre-war industrial locomotive. Hundreds of these were built, appearing first at army supply depots. After the war many were sold for industrial and colliery use.

In the USA the Railway Branch of the Corps of Engineers was responsible for locomotive design and procurement, until the formation of the US Transportation Corps in 1942. The designs produced in the pre-war period were unpromising, but in 1941

The German Kriegslok *locomotive, of which thousands were built for supplying the German army in occupied Europe, still survives in central Europe, its simplified maintenance being as attractive in peace as in war*

what was probably the most successful of the Allied war locomotives was designed. This was a 2-8-2, destined to become
known as the 'MacArthur' type, of which several hundred
examples are still at work in the Indian subcontinent. This design
originated when a British mission arrived in Washington to buy
locomotives for use on the Trans-Iranian Railway. The British
had intended to order fifty units of the First World War 'Pershing'
type 2-8-0, which had a good reputation. However, the US
Corps of Engineers regarded these as obsolete and, despite initial
British opposition, suggested a 2-8-2 design, which would have a
lighter axle weight, be easier on curves and have better steam-
raising capacity. A pair of locomotives built in 1924 by Baldwin
for the obscure Montana, Wyoming and Southern Railroad were
chosen as the basis of the new design. According to the engineer
officer who managed this project, Colonel Howard Hill, there
were all kinds of obstacles. The British, who had only with
reluctance been persuaded to accept the 'un-British' 2-8-2 wheel
arrangement, were equally reluctant to accept American practice
in the details. However, these objections were eventually solved,
even though compressed air sanding gear, with the sand stored in
an extra dome, was replaced by British-style steam sanding, with
the sandboxes close to the wheels. Even more troublesome than
British demands were the visits of salesmen from the various
American locomotive equipment firms. The design was worked
out just before America entered the war, when the equipment
suppliers were still suffering from the Depression and were
desperate for orders; although the initial British order had been
for fifty units this was soon increased, and it was realized that the
design might well be built in hundreds of units, making it the
biggest locomotive order in memory. As such, it promised to be a
bonanza for manufacturers of whichever superheaters, lubricators,
gauges, brakes and other parts were selected. In the end, besieged
by a stream of salesmen and unable to devote himself to the actual
work of designing the locomotive and drawing up its specification,
Colonel Hill isolated himself and refused to speak to salesmen.
The latter thereupon complained to their local congressman, or
to Engineer generals, men whom Colonel Hill could hardly
ignore. In the end, however, these pressures achieved nothing, and
the locomotives incorporated those components which their
designer considered most suitable. In all, 784 units were eventually
built in the USA and Canada. The first 200, built to British army

One of the American 'MacArthur' type locomotives at work in India. This was the most successful of the US war-service locomotives, and many are still at work

order, went to Iran, Egypt and elsewhere in the Middle East, while the remainder were ordered for the Indian railways.

Other US Army designs included a 2-8-0, which became very familiar on British railways in the months preceding the Normandy landings, after which it was transferred to the European continent. This design appears to have been prepared by a committee and, although it was quite suited to the poor track standards of the war-ravaged railways of Western Europe, it was not a great success, its lubrication system being primitive and its boiler having a tendency to explode. This malfunction was probably a result of a basic fault in the design, although manufacturing imperfections did occur in war-built locomotives.

Some of the MacArthur units, for example, had coupling rods that for some reason were about three-quarters of an inch too long.

The lessons of the First World War had been well learned by the American railroads, and there was no need for a government takeover to keep the traffic moving. The traffic was about double that carried in the First World War, but congestion was this time avoided. Traffic to the ports, whose delays had been the last straw in 1917, was successfully handled by a system in which freight awaiting shipment was unloaded and stored outside the ports; in principle, the railways only took into the ports freight for which ships were standing ready. Another difficulty of the First World War, the tendency of clients to delay the release of rolling stock, was largely avoided by the activities of voluntary shippers' committees, whose members would visit recalcitrant clients and persuade them, or shame them, into loading or unloading their cars faster. Most of the larger shippers took special measures to achieve this, often diverting scarce labour to loading operations. As a final inducement, the railroads had the right to impose an embargo on traffic moving to congested or laggard points. At no time was the US war effort hindered by railway transport difficulties. Indeed, at times the railroads performed better than even the optimists had expected. A widely publicized example was the emergency despatch of aircraft to replace the losses suffered at Pearl Harbor; forty-two carloads of aircraft being exported to Sweden were located by the railroads in New York docks, re-routed, and were ready and assembled in a Pacific port within a week. During the war as a whole, the railroads handled nine-tenths of the War Department's freight.

As in the First World War, line capacity was in excess of peacetime requirements, so the railroads were able to cope with vastly increased traffic. A notable surge in traffic followed the appearance of German submarines off the Eastern Seaboard in 1942. The tankers from the Gulf of Mexico that habitually carried oil to the eastern states soon disappeared and the railroads took over the traffic, at first using improvised equipment and procedures. A similar sequence occurred with the coal shipments from Virginian ports to New England.

Despite their distance from the battlegrounds, the US railroads also had a role in troop deployment, in the old European sense. Taking troops to embarkation ports was a considerable task, especially as the movements had to be made to suit port and shipping plans. Taking a leaf from the European book, modified freight cars were used to carry much of this traffic, because the existing passenger car stock was inadequate, especially for the long hauls from the eastern states to the Pacific ports. These emergency passenger vehicles resembled boxcars but were capable of running at passenger train speeds and were fitted with bunks; they were an improvement on the '40 men or 8 horses' tradition.

While freight traffic doubled on the US railroads, passenger traffic also reached an all-time peak in 1944. This was not altogether a blessing for the railroads. The overcrowded passenger trains, with their old rolling stock, frequent delays and slow schedules, made many Americans vow never to take the train again unless it was unavoidable.

In Canada the railways likewise carried greatly increased traffic. When German submarines made the Gulf of St Lawrence an unsafe sea route many ships were diverted from Quebec and Montreal to the eastern ports of Halifax and St John. This meant a longer rail haul for shipments, and a consequent increased demand for rolling stock. Not only this, but the lines to these ports were single track. Halifax, in particular, was poorly served by rail, for it had one link with the rest of Canada and with the USA, and this link was single track for 185 miles at its eastern end, with only occasional passing loops. Even in the First World War this situation had given trouble, so to avoid a repetition it was decided as early as 1941 to equip this threatened bottleneck with centralized train control. This enabled opposing trains to cross each other without delay. In fact, so neatly were train meets arranged from the control centre that it was possible for two trains to pass at loops without either having to stop. At times up to eighty trains could be passed in one day, although usually it was no more than fifty. The peaks occurred when US troops arrived to board the *Queen Elizabeth* or *Queen Mary* to travel to Britain. These ships could carry up to 14,000 soldiers, which meant that on the day of departure about twenty-eight special troop trains would draw into the Halifax ocean terminal, with each train being cleared and removed in little more than half an hour. After the war the process was reversed, this time with an even greater sense of urgency, because the troops were in no mood for delay.

For the French railways, the Second World War began very much like the First World War and the Franco–Prussian War. There were the same scenes at the Gare de l'Est, the same procession of military trains through the same regulating stations to the same receiving stations, except that some trains went somewhat farther in 1939 than they had in 1914, thanks to the recovery of the Alsace–Lorraine railways after 1918. However, all this changed in the early summer of 1940. As the German motorized troops poured into France, the Nord and Est regions of the SNCF found they had to interpose hundreds of evacuation trains among their military movements. As the Germans advanced farther the masses of people and equipment requiring a place on west-bound trains grew uncontrollably. Congestion developed, and was accentuated by heavy air attacks that cut essential lines. Bomb damage could always be repaired—preparations for heavier air attacks than these had been made well before the war—but even a few hours' hold-up could put the evacuation effort out of joint. One basic mistake was the attempted evacuation of all rolling stock; if the German advance had been slower this would have been a wise move, but in the conditions of 1940 long trains of empty freight cars seriously delayed the movement of loaded trains. This experience provided a useful lesson for others; a few weeks later, when Britain was expecting invasion, the British railwaymen were instructed to evacuate locomotives, but not empty rolling stock, in the event of an enemy landing.

In occupied France the railways came under German administration, with the former personnel retained. Exceptionally heavy military and naval traffic was hauled, but not in the directions envisaged by the peacetime planners. Immense quantities of building materials passed to the Channel coast and to the Atlantic ports and there was a continual flow of troop and naval specials. In the first years of the occupation there was little open resistance on the part of railway employees, but already there were railwaymen busy collecting information of military traffic movements, which was transmitted then to London, where it was collated to present a fairly accurate picture of German activity. Gradually, too, railway workers developed a taste for allowing things to go wrong, and then, when they had gone wrong, making them worse. Working to rule was an early and initial stage of this movement. Later a certain skill in making the most of small accidents, in the piling of delay upon delay, became

evident. Then there was the game of mis-documentation. Sometimes waybills would be lost, sometimes the labels on freight cars
changed *en route*. A consignment to the German forces labelled as
urgent was an attractive target for those who liked to send carloads of freight to the wrong destination. This mode of resistance
continued throughout the war, even though the Germans
intensified their supervision over railway operation.

When the Resistance became better organized, railwaymen
played a significant role. The French railway worker was a man
used to discipline, habituated to the concept of precise time-
keeping. Moreover his job gave him the chance to travel without
arousing any suspicions, and he was in an excellent position to

*A far cry from the less sophisticated, but equally effective, methods of rail
sabotage used by Sherman's troops in the American Civil War. This railway
bridge over the Maas River was blown up in 1940*

report on German activity, for he not only witnessed the passage of German trains but his travels took him past all kinds of military installations. It was only natural, therefore, that railwaymen should be employed as messengers between different Resistance groups, and as most valued informants. Also, when clandestine traffic grew to include messengers, fugitive Jews, Allied airmen, escaped prisoners-of-war and Resistance men on the run, the railwaymen played an essential role. The most celebrated exploit was the regular carriage of messengers into and out of occupied France in the tender water tank of the locomotive allocated to haul the special train of Pierre Laval, the collaborationist prime minister, between Paris and Vichy. Most Allied servicemen escaping to Spain travelled across France in passenger trains, relying on the silent co-operation of railway conductors and inspectors. A favourite service was the German mail train between Nantes and La Rochelle, which had a section for civilian traffic in which the Resistance could reserve an entire compartment for its repatriates, where they were unlikely to be troubled by talkative fellow-passengers.

From about 1943 sabotage began to take precedence over all activities except the information service. Sabotage took two forms; the classic derailment of trains in the countryside, and the more sophisticated disruption and destruction inside railway installations. The former was largely and increasingly undertaken by the Maquis guerillas, and railwaymen took a relatively small part. Many spectacular derailments were engineered, and in 1944 the Germans began to use armoured trains to escort particularly important trains or groups of trains, the idea being that an armoured train, closely followed by the escorted trains, could with impunity explode any mines and, furthermore, beat off the attacks which the Maquis often made on trains brought to a standstill.

Railwaymen, with their specific knowledge, were better employed at their place of work. Elementary actions included the incessant removal of electric bulbs in locomotive depots, making night work impossible, the misplacing of vital spare parts, and the practice on night troop trains of putting alternate shovelfuls of coal on the fire and on to the track so that a train could run out of fuel in mid-journey. Running a locomotive from its stall in a roundhouse into the turntable pit could immobilize that depot's locomotives for a day or more; later, when explosives became more plentiful, a charge beneath the turntable could wreak longer-lasting damage. Towards the end of the war, when the Germans had placed armed guards at all important installations, this kind of activity became difficult and was replaced by the armed attack from outside, culminating in sabotage after the German guard had been disposed of. Meanwhile, the German railway operating staff, drafted in increasing numbers from the German railways to both replace and watch over the SNCF personnel, and known by the latter derisively as '*bahnhofs*', was enlarged in early 1944 by a fresh levy of 25,000 skilled men, drafted in anticipation of a general railway strike. The '*bahnhofs*' did a good job in their operating role, but seemed to have played a very small part in uncovering or thwarting French Resistance activity; indeed, it is doubtful whether many of these German railwaymen were interested in getting involved in such tasks. Much more menacing were French informers, because even at the height of the struggle many Frenchmen were as interested in their personal quarrels as in the war against the Germans. During the war about 800 railwaymen were shot and another 1,150 sent to concentration camps from which they never returned. But this total loss of about 2,000 lives should be compared with the achievement of approximately 6,000 effective incidents of sabotage and about 1,400 derailments during the war.

In 1944 sabotage and derailments took an ever-more organized form. The general strategy was laid down in London, while the precise tactics were chosen by railwaymen, either acting alone or with the Maquis. Special plans were made for the expected Allied landings in Normandy. The Allied Supreme Command had decided that air attacks should be directed against German communications rather than against a few key industrial targets, and steps were taken to ensure that the Resistance should complete and supplement the destruction caused by the bombers. In previous months a certain pattern had been established. Since it seemed that bombers could not be relied on to hit any target smaller than a city, it was the Resistance which was entrusted with the task of immobilizing the French locomotive stock and destroying vital bridges after D-Day. In this way the reliability of French railwaymen as saboteurs actually reduced the destructiveness of war. For example, there was no plan to destroy by bombing the main stations and yards of Paris, because this would have involved the destruction of much of surrounding Paris and hundreds of lives. Instead, a few well-informed, brave railway-men, supplied with moderate quantities of explosives, were able to paralyse rail traffic in the Paris area.

In June 1944, railway transport all over France came to an almost complete halt as the saboteurs did their work. German reinforcements, sometimes arriving on French territory in 'armadas' of forty or fifty trains, were held up for days and even weeks, and only rarely ever reached their intended destination. Supply trains were immobilized by cutting both the entry and exit tracks of marshalling yards, while the sabotage of running lines was so finely planned that it was possible, on the approach of a block of German military trains, to cut one line ahead of it and then, each time it was re-routed, to cut the next line it took. An entire SS division *en route* to oppose the Normandy landings was delayed for two weeks in this way. German railway troops, using forced labour, worked hard, but were far too few to ensure any kind of reliable rail communication through France or, later, through Belgium and Holland.

The difficulty which aircraft experienced in hitting railway targets was glossed over during the Second World War, which is perhaps why its repetition during the Korean War seemed to come as a surprise. The Korean War, in the early 1950s, was possibly the last conflict in which railways were considered a decisive target. In this contest, in which the latest air and naval weapons were deployed against the railway system of North Korea, the railways emerged a clear winner. The Association of American Railroads, the pressure group representing the American railway companies, was so impressed by the per-formance of North Korean railwaymen, that it later published a free book, by General James Van Fleet, who had commanded the 8th Army in Korea. In this book the General recounted the great efforts he had made to destroy the North Koreans' supply rail-ways, and how he had failed. At a time when the US railroads were feeling the competition from subsidized highway and airline transport, the General's conclusions were especially welcome to his sponsors: 'Railway durability and recuperability have become thoroughly established as principles of military doctrine . . . military planners know that they must look to railroads for the great bulk of the military requirements for transport, in the future as in the past.'

In the early weeks of this war, the American and South

Korean forces thoroughly destroyed all railway bridges as they withdrew southwards. However, it was not long before the North Koreans had supply trains running. When the United Nations forces landed at Inchon to reverse the trend of the war, the North Korean supply lines were divided, as priority targets, between the US Air Force in the north-west and the Navy's ships and aircraft in the north-east. For about twenty months the North Korean railways were hammered by bombs, rockets and shells, but the trains still got through somehow. Having an inviolable base in China—which was out of bounds to UN bombers, and from where rolling stock could be drawn to replace losses—and having too an immense reservoir of manual labour, the North Korean transport managers were able to supply their forces throughout the war.

The aim of 'Operation Strangle', begun in August 1951, was to destroy the North Korean railways; this, it was estimated, would oblige the enemy to use a highway fleet of 6,000 motor trucks to do, less efficiently, what the railways had done with a stock of 600 boxcars. The intelligence estimates on which these calculations were based seem, in retrospect, to have been no more reliable than usual. By the end of August, after two weeks of intense attack, the railways did seem to falter, but this was largely because heavy rainfall had washed away some vital bridges. A small proportion of the bombs did find their targets, but as the North Koreans adapted themselves to a life of bombardment they developed methods that enabled them to repair a bombed line during the hours of darkness. If a bridge was destroyed too thoroughly to permit repair within eight hours, they built a new line and bridge to by-pass the wreckage. As European railway operators had discovered in a century of previous wars, it did not take long to restore damaged lines provided there were materials available. By the end of 1951 the US Air Force had decided that 'Operation Strangle' was an unprofitable employment for its medium bombers, and abandoned the project.

Three months later, in March 1952, a second attempt was made. This, 'Operation Saturate', was planned on the basis of the lessons learned the previous year. Since the North Koreans had managed to repair during the night lines that had been cut during the previous day, this time the bombing attacks were to be around the clock. Secondly, to make repair even more difficult only a few selected sections of line were to be attacked, the concentrated bombing being expected not only to damage the track but also to mutilate the whole sub-structure. However, this effort was little more successful than 'Operation Strangle'. An official Air Force history later commented ruefully: '. . . the medium bombers blasted and the Reds repaired in one continuous cycle.' In general, the operation failed because the tenacity of the North Koreans ensured that there were never quite enough bombers to do the job thoroughly. General Van Fleet described this assault: 'We dive-bombed and skip-bombed, we shelled with heavy naval guns, we cannonaded with ground artillery, we strafed with rockets and machine guns, we organized sabotage and guerilla attacks. But we never stopped the Red railroads from delivering ammunition and supplies. . . .'

One of the least unsuccessful attacks on the North Korean railways was against a six-span bridge between Kilchu and Songjin on the east coast main line, an operation that inspired the feature film 'The Bridges of Toko-ri'. The bridge was sixty feet high, 600 feet long, and built of steel and concrete. Crossing a ravine, it was entered at both ends through tunnels. Built originally by the Japanese, it had a duplicate set of piers alongside, and the tunnels also had duplicate bores. This arrangement was intended to facilitate the doubling of the railway in peacetime, or the quick replacement of damaged structures in wartime. However, the height of the bridge and the high ground on either side (making a by-pass very difficult) suggested to the U N command that it would be a suitably vulnerable target during 'Operation Saturate'.

In the first week of March 1952 the US Navy made three bomber attacks on this bridge, knocking out several spans. Within a week the Koreans had erected timber cribbing and the bridge was almost restored for traffic. Another attack was therefore made, which destroyed most of the cribbing and knocked out an additional span. At the end of March photo-reconnaissance showed that the cribbing had been restored and that the bridge was almost ready for traffic, so two more attacks were made. At the end of these the cribbing had gone, and only one span remained. At this point the North Koreans decided that they could not win at this particular game, so they began to build a four-mile by-pass line. This had eight small and low bridges instead of one long and high structure. The US Navy pilots managed to destroy these, but being of simple construction, they could be rebuilt almost overnight. Rather than allocate precious aircraft to these somewhat unrewarding attacks, the US Navy decided to seek promising targets elsewhere; the attacks had indeed blocked the line more or less completely for almost two months, but after the by-pass was built it was not possible to stop the trains running.

The cost in manpower of repairing the damage must have been enormous, but manpower was not short in North Korea. Various stratagems also helped the North Koreans to maintain their rail transport. At difficult periods the trains ran only during darkness, and were secreted in tunnels during the day. When lines were broken, a series of shuttle services was operated between the breaks; with ample labour the transhipment of freight from one train to another was quite feasible, although time-consuming. Sometimes they deceived aerial photography by laying debris and mud over the tracks, to suggest that bombs had cut the line; during the night these camouflages would be removed to allow the trains to run, and then they were replaced in time to be noticed by the next morning's reconnaissance flight. Sometimes bridge spans were removed in daytime, perhaps floated down a river to a tree-sheltered spot, or placed in nearby tunnels.

Meanwhile, the UN forces depended almost entirely on rail transport for the delivery of supplies from the South Korean ports. But what was particularly interesting was that in the west, where railways were plentiful, it was the Americans who did most of the fighting, daily receiving 600 tons of railborne supplies for each division. In the east and centre, where mountains and a poor railway network prevented any significant supply by rail, it was the South Korean forces which conducted the offensive; the South Koreans, like the Prussians in 1870, could fight their battles on a shoestring.

Of more recent wars, that in Vietnam was the most prolonged, but there railways played only a small part. Elsewhere in the world, the war in Eritrea, waged by local nationalists, did involve attacks on the sole railway in the region, and one successful blowing-up of a train appears to have resulted in heavy casualties. Much more interesting from the railway point of view was the war between India and Pakistan in 1971, which had many of the technical characteristics of previous European wars. Most interesting, although not yet fully elucidated, is the significance of railway-building for the actual start of hostilities. The Farakka railway crossing over the Ganges, which eliminated the most serious bottleneck on the route from India to the frontier of what was then East Pakistan, was opened in November. The war began in December. The manager of India's Eastern Railway, which performed the bulk of the transport service needed for this campaign, later wrote that without the Farakka crossing 'it would have been well-nigh impossible' to have moved the necessary troops and supplies.

The Eastern Railway ran about 500 special trains in the period leading up to the war and during the war itself, and this figure does not include over 100 ambulance trains. As the special trains could not avoid the Calcutta district, a number of passenger trains serving that city had to be cancelled to provide routes. In places the Railway was subject to sabotage by Pakistani raiders, and also, at two stations, to heavy shelling. In addition, a number of trains were damaged by mines.

When the Indian army entered East Pakistan its Territorial Army railway units handled most of the train operations, but Eastern Railway personnel were employed for the restoration of damaged routes. The most notable achievement of the latter was the laying of a supply railway of forty-three kilometres to link the Indian system with the Pakistani town of Jessore. Much of this was built over line built in British India, long since abandoned. The work took ten days, despite the presence of anti-tank mines and anti-personnel mines, which, being of plastic, were hard to locate. On another line, from Gede to Drasana, such mines twice caused numerous injuries to the Eastern Railway's labourers. A number of bridges, destroyed by the retreating Pakistanis, were also restored by reconstruction teams, using standard spans which were held in store by the Railway.

Thus in the Indo-Pak War, railways were important, but probably not decisive. This seems to reflect a modern trend. The railway no longer monopolizes mechanical transport; the road vehicle and the air-lift can to a large extent replace it, although at rather a heavy price in resources. The concept of rail-mounted artillery may possibly have a longer life, for at times both the USA and USSR have studied the feasibility of mounting nuclear rocket launchers on rail vehicles, thereby giving them a mobility that is far more protective than concrete.

Looking back over the decades to the 1830s, when the military significance of the railways began to be appreciated, it is difficult to resist the impression that railways were at no period quite so decisive an influence as had been forecast. The armoured train had a very limited career, the field railway could never adequately supply a major offensive, rapid railborne mobilization schemes by one power were answered by similar schemes on the part of their neighbours.

But while perhaps less decisive than anticipated in determining the outcome of wars, the railways did very much influence the nature of those wars. It was rail transport that sustained the mass armies and the mass participation of modern warfare. Total war was a product of the railway age, and without the railways would have been impossible.

Acknowledgements

Every effort has been made to contact the owners of the copyrights for the illustrations used in this book, and we apologize for any omissions caused through difficulty in tracing such sources. Acknowledgement is made for kind permission to use illustrations from the following sources:

Bildarchiv Preussischer Kulturbesitz, pp 62/63, 75

Imperial War Museum, pp 105, 106, 130/131, 136/137, 140, 154/155, 157, 159, 162, 166/167, 174

John Topham Picture Library, pp 184, 211

Library of Congress, pp 30/31, 33, 36/37, 44, 48/49, 52/53

Mansell Collection, pp 190/191, 202/203

National Railway Museum, pp 84/85, 172/173, 177, 187, 193

Robert Hunt Library, pp 98, 100/101

Vie du Rail, pp 67

Index